A Delight to All Who Know It
THE MAINE SUMMER ARCHITECTURE OF WILLIAM R. EMERSON
BY ROGER G. REED

Architectural Photography

by Richard Cheek

Maine Historic Preservation Commission

Augusta, Maine 1990

COVER:
Felsted, Frederick Law Olmsted Family Cottage, Deer Isle, by Richard Cheek

DESIGN:
Michael Mahan Graphics, Bath, Maine

TYPESETTING:
Black Spruce, Dresden Mills, Maine

PRINTING:
Penmor Lithographers, Lewiston, Maine

Printed under State appropriation 010 94P 1654 362

Library of Congress Catalog #90-063285

ISBN 0-935447-07-5

Redwood, Bar Harbor, sketch by John Calvin Stevens (Courtesy of John Calvin Stevens II)

There is an architect in this country,
whose beautiful domestic work,
scattered over a wide area
from Mt. Desert to Colorado Springs,
is a delight to all who know it.

Albert Winslow Cobb
Stevens & Cobb
Examples of American Domestic Architecture, 1889

Contents

THE PROJECTS: PART II

PROJECTS OUTSIDE MAINE

Foreword

The rugged natural beauty of the Maine coast has attracted summer visitors since before the Civil War. By the 1880s few coastal towns did not have at least one seasonal hotel and its attendant cottages. From York Harbor to Grindstone Neck summer colonies were established by Mainers as well as by those "from away." To record the history and architecture of these communities has been the focus of a continuing effort by the Maine Historic Preservation Commission. This has been accomplished through the support of National Park Service and state grants. Beginning in 1984, the Commission has conducted architectural surveys of Bar Harbor, Northeast Harbor, Seal Harbor, Southwest Harbor, Isle au Haut, Islesboro, Prout's Neck, Biddeford Pool, and Kennebunk Beach. Areas such as York Cliffs, Cape Arundel at Kennebunkport, and the Auburn Colony in South Harpswell have been listed in the National Register of Historic Places.

A major result of this concerted examination of Maine's summer heritage has been the discovery of a wealth of information about the architects and builders of cottages and hotels as well as their clients. From period newspapers, promotional brochures, photographs, blueprints, and deeds has emerged a more comprehensive picture of the economic, social, and cultural forces which shaped the Maine coast a century ago and which continue to influence it today. Architectural historian Roger G. Reed has been directly involved in this research effort since he joined the Commission's staff in 1983.

Early on Roger Reed identified William R. Emerson of Boston as one of the most innovative and distinctive architects to work on the Maine coast in the late nineteenth century. With Cynthia Zaitzevsky's 1969 study of Emerson as a foundation, Roger has spent countless hours reviewing survey data, reading original sources, locating rare pictorial material, and visiting surviving buildings. Using the basic tools of architectural survey, Roger has skillfully reconstructed the Maine career of one of the nation's most gifted practitioners of the Shingle Style. Through this publication, Emerson's work will once more become "a delight to all who know it."

Earle G. Shettleworth, Jr., Director
Maine Historic Preservation Commission

Acknowledgements

There is no collection of papers to document William R. Emerson's life and career. Consequently, research on the architect's work in Maine has been based largely upon nineteenth century newspapers, photographs, and drawings. I was assisted in this effort by Gladys O'Neil of the Bar Harbor Historical Society for commissions on Mt. Desert Island, Kim Lovejoy for those in Kennebunkport, and Earle G. Shettleworth, Jr., for numerous buildings from York to Blue Hill. Background information on Emerson begins with Cynthia Zaitzevsky's *The Architecture of William Ralph Emerson 1833-1917*, a 1969 catalogue that accompanied an exhibit at the Fogg Museum of Art, Harvard University. Although a great many projects have been identified since 1969, little new information has surfaced on Emerson's life.

Most of the illustrations are from the collection of the Maine Historic Preservation Commission. Several institutions and individuals have been helpful in providing photographs and drawings. Special thanks are due to Gladys O'Neil and Raymond Strout, both of Bar Harbor, who have supplied many important images. My deep appreciation is also due to the owners of Emerson buildings, who graciously gave me access into their homes. Finally, I want to thank Earle G. Shettleworth, Jr., without whose support this project would not have been accomplished.

Roger G. Reed

William Ralph Emerson, circa 1855 (Courtesy of Sylvia Watson).

William Ralph Emerson 1833-1917

The best examples of Maine's summer architecture compete with their breathtaking locations by evoking admiration for their architectural beauty. While historically there is an extraordinary variety in the character of structures built for summer use, those that stand out successfully exploit the natural beauty of a site without being viewed as an intrusion on the landscape. Many cottages built on the coast then, as now, appear out of place, and would sit more comfortably on a suburban street, unless you happen to be fortunate enough to be on the inside looking out. William Ralph Emerson succeeded better than most architects in creating a varied and fascinating range of designs which seem especially suited to Maine's rugged coastline. One of the first to note Emerson's ability to blend architecture and environment was Maria G. van Rensselaer, who wrote in 1886, "... while Mr. Emerson's house is throughly good as a house—as a dwelling-place for its own special owner— it also seems almost as much a part of nature's first intentions as do the rocks and trees themselves; to say that while it has material fitness that its site and its surroundings seem to have been designed for its sole sake and service."[1]

Of the one-hundred-sixty-one projects identified by this architect, forty-eight are in the Pine Tree State. The majority of these are summer cottages, while most of the remainder are related to summer resorts. Emerson's practice prospered at a time when the emergence of a leisure class and improvements in transportation enabled the most affluent Americans to summer in distant locations rather than simply dividing their time between the traditional city and suburban residences. Indeed, the transportation improvements allowed even the middle class to afford a summer cottage, if not in Bar Harbor, then in other, less prestigious locations. Recent research has shown that a great many major late nineteenth century architectural firms worked in Maine. Among these, William R. Emerson's work is outstanding, if for no other reason than that he is generally credited as the originator of the Shingle Style; and no other style is more associated with summer architecture on the Maine coast.[2]

It is a source of considerable frustration that so little is known about William R. Emerson, one of America's great architects. His only photograph is a daguerreotype, taken as a young man. He left no immediate family save a daughter-in-law, and no office records have survived. The basic facts of his life and career have been documented by Cynthia Zaitzevsky. He was born in Alton, Illinois in 1833, where his father, Dr. William S. Emerson, had moved to engage in land speculation. Dr. Emerson and his wife, Olive Bourne, were both from Kennebunk, Maine, and it was there that the widow returned in 1837 after her husband's death. Young William and his older brother Lincoln apparently spent much of their childhood in Boston living with their uncle, George B. Emerson. Both brothers received their early education in Boston public schools.[3] There was a significant difference in the educational opportunities afforded the young men. Lincoln Fletcher (born 1829) became a protegee of his uncle, a noted educator. He attended Bowdoin College from 1845 to 1849, graduating with highest honors. A year of studying medicine in Boston followed, but he gave that up to teach and work as an assistant to his uncle. In 1854 Lincoln went abroad for two years of study and travel, then returned to open a school for young ladies in Boston. In contrast, William Ralph was evidently left to his own devices to pursue a career.[4]

William R. Emerson's training, however, was quite typical for the period. He first entered the employ of Jonathan Preston, an architect-builder in Boston. According to city directories he worked for Preston as early as 1854, becoming a partner in 1857.[5] The firm of Emerson & Preston lasted until 1861. As a young draftsman in Preston's office, he worked on the Boston Theater of 1854. The only project identified from the Preston and Emerson partnership is a row of four elegant marble fronted townhouses still standing on Hancock Street. These structures, built in 1859, were the first in the city to feature a facade of marble veneer.[6]

During the early 1860's Emerson practiced under his own name for a few years, then formed a partnership with Carl Fehmer in 1864. During that nine year association the firm of Emerson & Fehmer designed several Back Bay townhouses as well as the M. H. Sanford House in Newport, Rhode Island. The fact that Carl Fehmer was a successful and stylish architect in his own right makes it highly problematical to distinguish his contribution to a project from that of Emerson.

In 1867 Emerson became a charter member of the Boston Society of Architects, and on May 21, 1869, he gave a talk on the importance of Colonial architecture in New England. At about the same time he was engaged in restoration work on the Old Ship Meeting House in Hingham, Massachusetts. These activities reflect the origins of a life-long interest in American Colonial architecture which had a profound influence on his work.

By 1874 Emerson was again on his own. The architect's projects for the remainder of the 1870's were characteristic of prevailing stylistic fashions and included the High Victorian Gothic Massachusetts Homeopathic Hospital of 1874-76 and the Stick Style Forbes House in Milton of 1876. At least one major commission, however, defies stylistic categorization. This is the William Ellery Channing Eustis House in Milton of 1877-78, a stone residence that is one of the architect's most important projects. This extraordinary house is distinguished both for its free interpretation of prevailing styles and its imaginative open floor plan. With this project Emerson refined his skills at planning seasonal homes for the wealthy. From 1879, the year of his first major work in Maine, until his retirement about 1909, Emerson increasingly specialized in country residences and summer cottages.

Four draftsmen who worked for Emerson and later became architects have been identified. William E. Barry, who shared Emerson's love for American Colonial architecture and Maine antecedants, worked for him in the mid-1860s.[7] Charles A. Rich was employed as a draftsman and delineator from 1876 until 1881, when he moved to New York City to form the firm of Lamb & Rich.[8] That partnership enjoyed considerable popularity designing numerous Shingle Style homes on the East Coast. During much of the 1880s Albert Winslow Cobb took Rich's place as principal delineator, providing a striking continuity in rendering style. Cobb, one of Emerson's most reverential admirers, was in partnership with John Calvin Stevens in Portland from 1888 to 1891 and later practiced in Springfield, Massachusetts.[9] From 1889 to 1891 Jarvis Hunt, a nephew of the architect Richard Morris Hunt and the artist William M. Hunt, served as Emerson's draftsman before attending the Massachusetts Institute of Technology. In 1893 Hunt moved to Chicago, where he became a successful architect.[10] In addition, Emerson's son, Ralph Lincoln, worked for his father from 1896 until his death in 1898. During his short life, he designed at least two buildings in his own right.[11]

This outline of Emerson's career tells us nothing about the man. In large part this may be due to the series of personal tragedies which left so little family to survive him. In addition to his father's death in 1837, his brother died of consumption in 1864 and left no children. William's first wife, Catherine Mears, died after less than ten years of marriage. A daughter by his second wife died after one year, and his son Ralph succumbed to tuberculosis as a young man. Sylvia Watson, his second wife and an accomplished artist, died a few months before the architect.

A few scattered comments made by those who knew him do nothing to contradict Frederick Law Olmsted, Jr.'s 1941 description of Emerson as "a talented but somewhat eccentric Boston architect".[12] Olmsted made a similar comment in 1896 during the construction of Felsted, the family summer home on Deer Isle. He reported to his mother that "John and I went to dinner at the Emersons last night and talked about the house and other things. He had made some sketches that were very pretty (I didn't agree with the plan of course). He is joyfully unbusinesslike isn't he? But I think he will make the house a pretty one."[13] John Calvin Stevens, the distinguished Maine architect of the Shingle Style, recalled: "I can never forget the friendly manner and interest displayed by William R. Emerson whose work and words were an inspiration. His office was in the same building and the fine fellows in that office took me in as almost

Sylvia Watson Emerson, circa 1860 (Courtesy of Sylvia Watson).

Ralph Lincoln Emerson, 1891
(Courtesy of the Harvard University Archives).

one of themselves."[14] Two Boston architects also provided comments on Emerson the man. Albert Winslow Cobb's encomium that appeared in *Examples of American Domestic Architecture* (and forms the title of this book) concludes by stating that "Now this man's work is lovely, because there is instilled into it the power of a chivalrous, joyous nature, revering everything pure and brave and holy in his fellow creatures, while scorning all that is extravagant, meretricious."[15] An intriquing description by another contemporary, William D. Austin, combines with Cobb's view to suggest a charismatic character: "One's recollection of him is rather 'hazy'. As a fact Mr. Emerson didn't figure prominently in the meetings of the Society but whenever he did say something or read a paper, he always held his audience by the vigor of his presentation and the picturesque quality of his language."[16]

Austin's comments were made in 1944, long after the Boston Society of Architects passed the "Resolutions on the death of William Ralph Emerson" in 1918. This extraordinary tribute remains unsurpassed as a eulogy to the architect:

Through the death of William Ralph Emerson, the Boston Society of Architects loses one of its earliest and best loved members. Mr. Emerson was a native product of New England, delighting in ingenious contrivances and original inventions, filled with enthusiasms for whatever was spontaneous and natural, and abhorring conventions of every sort. He was the creator of the shingle country house of the New England coast, and taught his generation how to use local materials without apology, but rather with pride in their rough and homespun character. He was keenly alive to the picturesque in nature and in art, and sketched unceasingly in the most charming way, often with strange tools and methods of his own devising. To his friends and pupils he was a source of inspiration, a unique personality, not shaped in the schools, a lover of artistic freedom. Though of late years Mr. Emerson has seldom been present at meetings of this Society, he has not been absent from the memories of those who knew him in the earlier days of his activity. Only they can justly estimate the great value of his influence in liberating architectural design from artificiality and in making simple and natural means artistically effective.[17]

While these sources extol Emerson as a free spirit, it is also true that he actively sought publication of his work, including allowing its use in advertising building products for Dexter Brothers and Samuel Cabot stains.[18] Indeed, the large number of published drawings and photographs are a principal source of documentation for his career. It is through these illustrations that we can document the range of the man's achievements, for, as with any architect, some projects do nothing to enhance his reputation for originality and creativity.[19] While his designs were popular, Emerson made the most of it in securing wealthy clients. When such clients no longer sought him out in great numbers, he contented himself with smaller projects and his paintings. The death of his son in 1898 may have contributed to an apparent inclination at the end of his career to publish his impressionistic paintings rather than drawings or photographs of completed projects.[20]

Redwood, Bar Harbor, perspective view by Charles Rich, *American Architect and Building News*, March 22, 1879
(Courtesy of the Archives, Society for the Preservation of New England Antiquities).

Emerson's Work in Maine: An Overview

The projects of William R. Emerson in Maine are representative of the architect's best work from 1879 until the end of the century. The major commissions are presented chronologically. The first part includes buildings for which illustrations or architectural drawings are available. They are followed by a second group of projects, again arranged chronologically, for which illustrative material or adequate documentation is lacking.

The year 1879 was pivotal in the development of Emerson's career and of the mode for which he is most often associated, the Shingle Style. That was the year in which Redwood, the Bar Harbor cottage of Charles J. Morrill, was built. Redwood was among the first major examples of the new concepts in interior planning and exterior ornament which came to dominate the decade of the 1880s.[21] These changes were elucidated by art critic Maria G. van Renssellaer in an important article, "American County Dwellings", published in 1886:

For a long time the most usual pattern in our country homes [was to] build a rectangular box with a straight 'entry' through the middle and two square rooms on each hand. If greater size was desirable, we added other rooms and 'entries' on this side and on that, but gave the plan no center, no coherence, and no nicety of convenience or charm of architectural effect.

This situation had improved of late, as she went on to describe:

But now in homes of every size the tendency is to make the hall at once beautiful and useful, the most conspicuous feature in the architectural effect and the most delightful living-room of all; not a living room like the others, but one with a distinct purpose and therefore a distinct expression of its own. In our climate and with our social ways of summer-living, we absolutely require just what it can give us—a room which in its uses shall stand midway between the piazzas on the one hand and the drawing-rooms and libraries on the other; perfectly comfortable to live in when the hour means idleness, easy of access from all points outside and in, largely open to breeze and view, yet with a generous hearthstone where we may find a rallying-point in days of cold and rain.... Not only the hall itself but the whole house profits by this alteration. It supplies what was lacking before, a logical center to the most extended and complicated design. It makes grouping possible; it divides and yet converts the various apartments; *it unifies the plan while permitting it a far greater degree of variety than was possible with the old box-like scheme* (emphasis added).[22]

Understanding these developments is critical to appreciating the changes in house plans developed by Emerson and other architects during the late 1870s. Typical of the picturesque summer cottages of that decade was a scheme

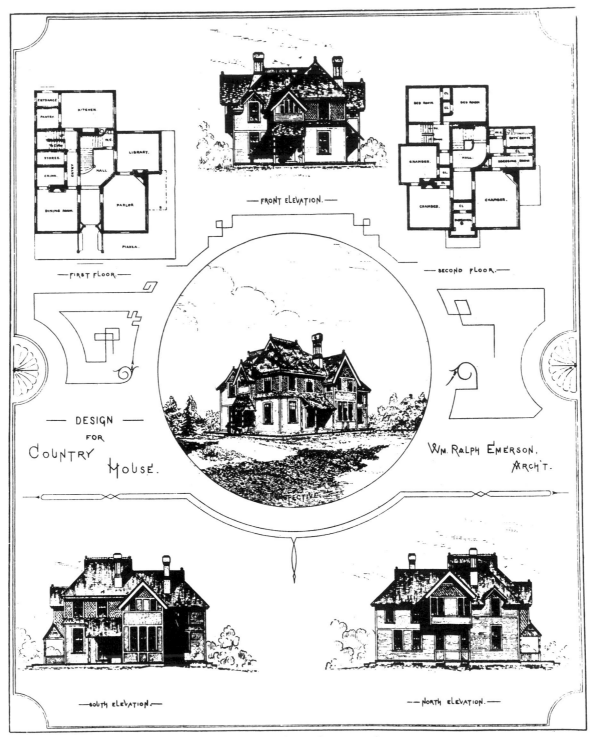

Design for Country House, *Architectural Sketch Book*, November, 1876
(Courtesy of Earle G. Shettleworth, Jr.).

Emerson contributed to the *Architectural Sketch Book* in November of 1876. His "Design for a County House" is confused and awkward with an asymmetrical exterior superimposed around a rather boxey plan with a central hall. The contrast with the design for Redwood, published three years later, cannot be more striking, especially as both schemes appear to have provided about the same number of rooms. The fact that Redwood in perspective view looks considerably larger reveals much about its more open and easily accessible internal arrangements.

One of the elements most often noted about Redwood is the fact that the exterior is fully shingled from roof to just above grade level. For this reason, the architect is credited with "inventing" the Shingle Style.[23] Rather than assigning Emerson such credit on the basis of a single published design, it is perhaps more useful to consider the astonishing variety of Shingle Style designs eminating from his hand throughout the 1880s. Within a few years he literally explored every variety of decorative effort possible with shingles. Many of the architect's projects were built in Maine and most of these in Bar Harbor. The earliest examples exhibited ornamental influences derived from the English Queen Anne style of British architect Richard Norman Shaw. As early as 1880, however, Emerson began to dress his shingled designs with ornament derived from the American Colonial Revival. St. Sylvia's Catholic Church of 1880 followed Redwood by substituting Colonial Revival style ornamentation for Queen Anne and extended the shingling to the interior walls.

Throughout the 1880s the Bar Harbor newspapers noted the arrival of the famous Bostonian in town, and his work dominated much of the architectural character of cottage construction during those years. Typical was the comment in the *Bar Harbor Tourist*: "Mr. William R. Emerson, the great architect of Bar Harbor, is rusticating at the Ocean House."[24] From 1881 to 1883 he designed eleven major summer cottages. These included Thirlstane and Mossley Hall, two of the architect's most admired projects. Other cottages followed on coastal sites as far south as Kittery. In addition, there were other types of structures associated with summer resorts, including four more churches.

An abrupt change in Emerson's prominence as the architect for affluent cottage builders occurred in the 1890s following a growing demand among the wealthiest clients for larger, more formal mansions built in traditional European styles. Frequently these buildings were of masonry construction with landscaped gardens. Emerson obtained a few such projects in places like Newport, Rhode Island, and New London, Connecticut, but he was no longer a leading architect for the exceptionally wealthy. This was especially true of Bar Harbor, but also characterized what was happening along much of the Maine coast. For those who preferred something less ostentatious, such as Thomas

Baily Aldrich or the Frederick Law Olmsted family, Emerson was sought out. His later work tended to rely more on simple Colonial motifs dressed in plain square-cut shingles. The gambrel roof was frequently employed as the most effective method to exploit the full potential of exterior shingling.

Generally, the smaller, more conventionally styled buildings Emerson designed in the 1890s are less admired by architectural historians than his larger, more exuberant work of the 1880s. These judgements are perhaps unfair in light of his evolving philosophy which the architect expounded in an 1899 article titled, "The Elimination of the Superfluous". "The tendency of the age", Emerson wrote, "is towards useless, senseless, meaningless elaboration." He went on to assert that, "It is fortunate that the old New England builders never had a French training, but were brought up on the old 'Builder's Guides', and did before Caesar Daly had flooded the literature of the art with voluminous unhealthiness, and that Charles Bulfinch studied the works of Sir Christopher Wrenn and Sir William Chambers and ignored the French masters altogether."[25] The simplicity of treatment in Emerson's late work should be understood as a deliberate and consistent evolution of his philosophy rather than a decline in his own abilities. Work such as Felsted on Deer Isle must be viewed in this light as a culmination of his career.[26]

Previously Unpublished Emerson Drawings

This publication features several previously unpublished architectural drawings. The lack of surviving records from Emerson's firm makes any of his drawings rare. For the Maine projects, the following have been located:

Beau Desert, Bar Harbor, 1881. Two exterior elevations and two floor plans, ink on linen. Gerrish Collection, Jessup Memorial Library, Bar Harbor.

Thomas D. Blake Cottage, Castine, 1891. Blueprints of four exterior elevations, three floor plans, and a foundation plan. Private Collection. In addition, the Maine Historic Preservation Commission has a drawing for a china cabinet in the Blake Cottage, graphite on heavy paper.

Blue Hill Inn, 1891. Four exterior elevations of the Inn on three sheets, ink on linen; two exterior elevations of the Engine House, graphite on tissue; details of six interior elevations of the Inn, graphite on heavy paper; detail of fireplace andirons, watercolor on heavy paper. There are also several miscellaneous full-scale detail drawings, graphite on heavy paper. Blue Hill Historical Society Collection.

E. W. Mayo House, Blue Hill, 1892. Four exterior elevations on three sheets, graphite, ink and watercolor on heavy paper. Maine Historic Preservation Commission Collection.

The Crags, Thomas Baily Aldrich Cottage, Tenant's Harbor, 1893. Blueprints of three exterior elevations and floor plans. Private Collection.

Felsted, Deer Isle, 1896. Blueprints of four exterior elevations, two floor plans, foundation plan, roof plan; sunprints of preliminary floor plans; garden plan, ink on heavy paper; porch and garden wall elevations, graphite on tissue. Collection of the Frederick Law Olmsted National Historic Site, Brookline, Massachusetts.

Charles P. Clark House Additions, Kennebunkport, 1898. Blueprints for four exterior elevations and three floor plans. Kennebunkport Historical Society Collection.

These drawings reveal some information about the architect's techniques in preparing working drawings. Emerson's style was not that of the precise, measured elevation drawings that were typical of Ecole des Beaux Arts trained architects and became standard by the early 1900s. William R. Emerson's 1889 article for *Technology Architectural Review*, ''Freehand Drawing'', expressed some of his sentiments toward architectural drafting:

"A proficiency in freehand drawing is indispensable in the daily practice of an architect's office. The cases are very rare in which time enough can be given to the preparation of elaborate mechanical perspective drawings; but there is an almost hourly need of such ready freehand representations of the work in hand as will serve for study on the part of the architect himself, and for a better understanding of it on the part of the client."[27] He went on to state that ". . . let him boldly feel his way through his work without any thought as to whether it will be a pretty picture or otherwise, so it be a fair, honest expression of the thought in his mind."[28]

These sentiments seem to apply to the elevation drawings which survive for his Maine projects as well as to the pictures which he painted toward the end of his career. As Cynthia Zaitzevsky has pointed out, this article reveals Emerson's own philosophy, which emphasized self-training through practice over rigorous academic education in developing drafting skills. Regrettably, the small selection of drawings featured here is too limited to more than suggest characteristics of Emerson's drawing techniques. It can be hoped that in the future additional drawings will be located in order to allow for a more comprehensive analysis.

NOTES

1. Maria G. van Rensselaer, "American Country Dwellings", *The Century Magazine*, Vol. XXXII, June, 1886, pp. 209-210. The reference here is to the Mary Hemenway Cottage in Manchester, Massachusetts, but it applies to much of the architect's work.

2. Contemporary architectural historians owe much to Vincent Scully, whose work, *The Shingle Style*, Yale, 1955, brought the Shingle Style in general, and William Ralph Emerson in particular, to the attention of scholars and laymen alike. This was followed by *The Architecture of William Ralph Emerson 1833-1917* by Cynthia Zaitzevsky, Harvard University, 1969. Dr. Zaitzevsky's monograph on Emerson was of inestimal value to me both for her excellent research and her critical understanding of the architect's work.

3. Zaitzevsky, *Emerson, op. cit.*

4. Letter from Mrs. O. L. B. Lord to Professor Packard, April 6, 1888, Bowdoin College Archives. There is in this documentation the suggestion of some bitterness on William's part toward his brother. Mrs. Lord (his mother's name after remarriage) wrote to answer an inquiry concerning her eldest son's career, to which William had failed to reply to after almost ten years.

5. According to one source, Emerson became a co-partner of Preston's in 1853 at age 20. While there is no other evidence that he became a partner that early, 1853 is probably the year he went to work for Preston. *Illustrated Boston The Metropolis of New England*, New York, 1889, p. 153.

6. For Emerson's participation in the plans for the Boston Theater, see *Illustrated Boston, op. cit.* A brief description of the Hancock Street townhouses appeared in the *Architects and Mechanics Journal*, New York, Vol. I, October, 1859, p. 5.

7. Kevin Murphy, "William E. Barry", *A Biographical Dictionary of Architects in Maine*, Vol. I, No. 6, 1984.

8. For example, Rich was the delineator of the perspective view of Redwood, which was published in the *American Architect and Building News* on March 22, 1879. The Boston directories document that Rich worked for Emerson.

9. John Calvin Stevens and Albert Winslow Cobb, *American Domestic Architecture*, Watkins Glen, New York, 1978; reprint of the 1889 publication with an introduction by Earle G. Shettleworth, Jr. and William D. Barry.

10. Information found in Boston directories.

11. Zaitzevsky, *op. cit.*, p. 89.

12. Frederick Law Olmsted, Jr. to Mrs. C. L. Pashley, August 22, 1941, copy in Maine Historic Preservation Commission files, Augusta.

13. Frederick Law Olmsted, Jr. to Mother, June 10, 1896, Olmsted Papers, Library of Congress, Washington, D. C.

14. Undated draft of letter to Hubert G. Ripley, Collection of John Calvin Stevens II. The letter refers to the brief period in the early 1880s when John Calvin Stevens managed a Boston office for the Portland firm of Fassett & Stevens.

15. John Calvin Stevens and Albert Winslow Cobb, *Examples of American Domestic Architecture*, New York, 1889, p. 30.

16. William D. Austin, " A History of the Boston Society of Architects in the Nineteenth Century", 1942, unpublished manuscript in the Boston Athenaeum, Chapters 2, 3. Cited in Zaitzevsky, *op. cit.*, p. 30.

17. January Meeting, Boston Society of Architects, January 8, 1918. These resolutions were forwarded to the American Institute of Architects, which published them in their *Journal* in 1918. Vincent Scully reproduced them from that source in his *Shingle Style, op. cit.*, p. 111, n. 62.

18. The architect's arrangements with Samuel Cabot may not have included more than an endorsement, such as the one accompanying a sketch by an unidentified architect in *Building*, Vol. X, 1889. His association with Dexter Brothers, however, was more long-lasting. The following examples have been identified:
The Brochure Series of Architectural Illustrations, Vol. I, 1895: Mossley Hall, Bar Harbor; Beau Desert, Bar Harbor; Lowell House, Chestnut Hill, Massachusetts; Parkinson Cottage, Bourne, Massachusetts; Eustis House, Newport, Rhode Island.
Inland Architect and News Record, June, 1896: Parkinson Cottage, Bourne, Massachusetts.
The Architectural Review, Vol. IV, 1896-97: Fair Haven, Kennebunkport.
Catalogue, Special Exhibition, Boston Architectural Club, 1897: Lowell House, Chestnut Hill, Massachusetts.
Inland Architect and News Record, November, 1897: Eustis House, Newport, Rhode Island.
Inland Architect and News Record, January, 1900: Mossley Hall, Bar Harbor.
Catalogue of the Architectural Exhibition, Boston Architectural Club, 1902: Unitarian Church, Bar Harbor.
Advertisement from unidentified architectural journal, n.d.: Rock Ledge, Kennebunkport.

19. For a particularly egregious Emerson design, see "House at Swampscott, Massachusetts", *The Engineering Record*, July 18, 1891.

20. See entry on Joseph L. Curtis Cottage, n. 3.

21. Cynthia Zaitzevsky has discussed the importance of Emerson's William E. C. Eustis House in Milton of 1877-78 for its fine open plan and as a precursor to Redwood's room arrangements. See Zaitzevsky, *op. cit.*, pp. 5-7.

22. van Rensselaer, *op. cit.*, pp. 215-216.

23. Scully and Zaitzevsky credit Emerson as the originator of the Shingle Style. Both scholars cite the principal nineteenth century source for this attribution as architect Bruce Price. Price singled out Emerson in his article "The Suburban House", *Scribner's Magazine*, Vol. VIII, No. 1, July, 1890, p. 18.

24. *Bar Harbor Tourist*, August 17, 1881.

25. William R. Emerson, "The Elimination of the Superfluous", *The Architectural Review*, November, 1899, p. 142. Emerson unfavorably compares several buildings around Copley Square to the Boston Public Library. These unnamed buildings are the Museum of Fine Arts (1870, Sturgis & Brigham) and New Old South Congregational Church (1874, Cummings & Sears) as well as his own Boston Art Club (1881-82). The terra cotta in the latter structure he calls "baked ugliness".

26. Emerson's late work has received virtually no attention. Included in this period were several unusual urban dwellings in places such as Cincinnati, Ohio; Chicago, Illinois; and Hartford, Connecticut. These and other projects require more indepth investigation to fully understand the architect's career.

27. William Ralph Emerson, "Freehand Drawing", *Technology Architectural Review*, Department of Architecture, Massachusetts Institute of Technology, Vol. III, No. 5, September 7, 1889, p. 25.

28. *Ibid.*

Redwood, land side, circa 1885 (Maine Historic Preservation Commission).

Redwood, Charles J. Morrill Cottage

Charles J. Morrill, a Boston financier, probably received his introduction to Bar Harbor through his partner, Alpheus Hardy, the first cottage builder there.[1] Morrill chose a semi-isolated shorefront site not far from where three other Bostonians had plans to build: Professor J. B. Thayer, Mrs. Rodman Rotch, and Lucien Carr. Redwood, which was named for red maples on the lot, has become one of the most architecturally significant summer cottages in Maine. It was Emerson's first major Shingle Style design and established his credentials as a leading architect of summer residences in New England.

Redwood acquired its reputation following the publication of the design in the *American Architect and Building News* on March 22, 1879.[2] The inspiration for Redwood clearly derives from the work of British architect Richard Norman Shaw. This is evident both in the Queen Anne style ornamentation and in Charles Rich's rendering style. A more direct inspiration may be Shaw's design for "Merriest Wood", published in the London journal *Building News* on May 25, 1877.[3] There is a general similarity between the two houses in that the principal elevations of both designs are rectangular with wings at acute angles and an entrance portico beneath a projecting gable-roofed pavilion. Moreover, Shaw's design employs traditional English building elements in the same way that Emerson was influenced by traditional American structures. Merriest Wood featured vernacular Tudor half-timbering without the English Renaissance influence found in Shaw's more famous work. Similarly, Emerson's use of shingling was derived from American vernacular buildings of the seventeenth and eighteenth centuries. In this sense Redwood is an American counterpart to Merriest Wood. A major difference between the two architects is that the New Englander continued to exploit the potential of American vernacular, whereas the Britan's work evolved toward grand Georgian mansions.

Redwood (Richard Cheek).

Redwood, ocean side, *American Architect and Building News*, March 22, 1879
(Courtesy of the Archives, Society for the Preservation of New England Antiquities).

As has been pointed out by Zaitzevsky, the house as constructed differed in many details from the published design. The contrast is most evident in comparing that rendering to one made by Portland architect John Calvin Stevens in 1883.[4] The high stone foundation as built, which was probably due to ledge, spoiled the intention to carry the exterior shingling down to just above the ground level. This also resulted in the veranda being elevated above the ground in a traditional fashion. As originally envisioned, the octagonal veranda appeared to suggest a tent-like pavilion rather than a porch. This extraordinary attempt to visually diminish the impact of the veranda does not seem to have been tried in many other projects.[5]

There are other differences between the design and the house as built, but the major discrepancy has to do with the proportions of Rich's perspective view which make the house look larger than it was. In fact, Redwood is not a particularly big cottage. Its much admired floor plan is exceptionally simple and open with the three principal rooms—hall, parlor and dining room—radiating off the entry hall. The hall is perhaps the most novel feature of the plan, for it is at an intermediate level between the first and second floors and acts as an enlarged staircase landing. It is large enough, however, to have a fireplace, a balcony overlooking the parlor, and a door for the exterior stairs to the veranda. These room arrangements are a model of convenience and ease of access, the hallmark of a summer cottage.

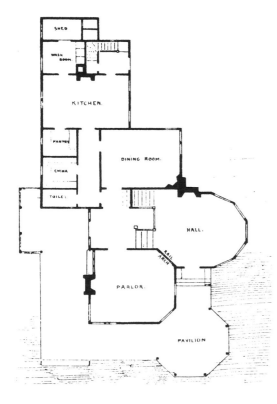

Redwood Stable, 1883 sketch by John Calvin Stevens (Courtesy of John Calvin Stevens II).

Redwood, first floor plan, *(AABN)*.

Redwood, entrance hall and staircase (Richard Cheek).

The ocean side of the house is more informal and has never received as much attention, as it was not intended to be seen in the same manner as the land facade. Only guests permitted to stroll upon the lawn or those passing by in their yacht would see it, and even then the primary focus of their attention would be the scenery, not the house. This point is important in understanding the design of many of Emerson's Bar Harbor cottages, where general access was not available on the water side. In the case of Redwood, it is also the water side that has received the most alterations, particularly with the staircase and veranda being enclosed. The only major changes to the interior are the remodeling of the first floor of the servants' wing, including the creation of a study out of the pantry and china closet.

A carriage house and a laundry designed by Emerson became a separate property when they were converted into residences. The best view of the former in its original design is found in a John Calvin Stevens sketch.[6]

1. At the end of his career, Charles J. Morrill became treasurer of the Provident Institution for Savings and a trustee for the Augustus Hemenway estate. Morrill may have come to know Emerson through Mary Hemenway, who provided the architect with at least four major commissions. In 1882 Morrill evidently planned another summer cottage on Isle au Haut, where there was a summer colony founded by landscape architect Ernest W. Bowditch. Bowditch was Mary Hemenway's son-in-law.

2. *American Architect and Building News*, Vol. V, No. 169, March 22, 1879. The documentation for the actual construction date of Redwood is *The Ellsworth American*, February 19, 1880.

3. *Building News*, London, May 25, 1877.

4. John Calvin Stevens Sketch Book, Collection of John Calvin Stevens II. Like his partner Albert Winslow Cobb, Stevens was a great admirer of Emerson's work. His sketch book also includes drawings of Emerson houses in the Boston area.

5. This porch treatment was successfully employed on Emerson's John Parkinson Cottage at Buzzard's Bay, Massachusetts of circa 1886.

6. *Op. cit.*, Stevens Sketch Book.

Redwood, detail of west elevation (Richard Cheek).

Church of St. Sylvia, sketch by John Calvin Stevens dated September 17, 1883 (Courtesy of John Calvin Stevens II).

Church of St. Sylvia

Two Philadelphians, DeGrasse Fox and Brooke White, were responsible for having this Catholic church built on land they provided near the Malvern Hotel. Emerson donated the plans, and the date of the design was 1880, as work began late that winter.[1] Fox, a developer and architect-builder who played a major role in Bar Harbor's transformation into a resort, acted as contractor. The first service was held in July, 1881, although the church was not consecrated until August, 1882.

St. Sylvia is one of Emerson's most admired projects. He published a perspective view of the church in the *American Architect and Building News* on June 25, 1881. John Calvin Stevens sketched it in 1883, as did Arnold Brunner in 1884.[2] A sketch also appeared in Mrs. van Rensselaer's article "Recent Architecture in America", which appeared in *Century Magazine* for January, 1885. The exterior was entirely shingled, which was unusual for a church, but the real importance of the design is as an expression of American Colonial Revival architecture which avoided mimicking the traditional eighteenth century meeting house. At a time when congregations usually built highly picturesque churches inspired by European styles such as the Gothic or Romanesque, St. Sylvia stood as a quiet interpretation of American vernacular traditions. The most prominent feature is the bell tower, inspired by the Old Ship Meeting House in Hingham, Massachusetts. The informal, almost medieval character of the design is emphasized by the manner in which classical motifs, such as the pediments and porch arches, are employed with great restraint.

The interior was shingled as well. According to a local newspaper, "the idea came to Mr. Fox, while reading that churches were so finished in the most northern countries of Europe. The thought was at once acted upon. It is likely to meet with much favor here and become popular through the Country, as architects are much taken with the idea."[3] As originally built, the church had a capacity for 300, but within a few years Bar Harbor's rapid growth necessitated an enlargement. In 1886 the nave was cut in two, presumably just in front of the altar, with the end section moved by fifteen feet to allow the construction of an in-fill containing 100 pews. Photographs of the church taken after the changes show very little evidence of an alteration.[4]

1. *Mt. Desert Herald*, August 15, 1882.
2. Stevens Sketch Book; *Building*, Vol. III, No. 1, October, 1884.
3. *Bar Harbor Tourist*, July 2, 1881.

4. *Bar Harbor Record*, May 26, 1887. Another Emerson church in the same idiom as St. Sylvia is St. Margaret's Catholic Church in Beverly, Massachusetts, still standing in an excellent state of preservation. St. Sylvia's was replaced with a large stone structure in the Romanesque style.

The Briars, southeast view, circa 1890 (Courtesy of Raymond L. Strout).

The Briars, J. Montgomery Sears Cottage

J. Montgomery Sears became one of the wealthiest men in Boston through his real estate interests. As a ward of Alpheus Hardy, he would have visited Bar Harbor in the first decade of its development as a summer resort. He also would have known Charles Morrill, Hardy's partner, and Redwood. Sears purchased a choice lot between the Hardy and Morrill Cottages at the beginning of the real estate boom of the 1880s and began construction in March, 1881[1].

Emerson again shingled the exterior, although in this instance he created almost seamless exterior walls, even covering the chimney below the roof line as well as to the ground just above grade in the manner intended for Redwood. The use of shingles here enabled the Queen Anne style ornament to stand out in sharp relief. The only photographs of this cottage are from the southeast. They reveal that the carriage entrance was from the side and that the principal elevation faced the water. The reason for this orientation was due in part to the fact that the Briars stood on the shore path along the ocean, allowing for a public view of that side.[2]

Sears hired Emerson to enlarge the stable in 1884. Further additions were made in 1890, including a bowling alley.[3] It is not known if Emerson was the architect for these improvements. However, he clearly did design the servants' house, which probably dates from 1881. This structure is typical of Emerson's fanciful small outbuildings which can be considered equivalent to the architectural "follies" found on English estates.

A playhouse built in 1898 was designed by Andrews, Jacques & Rantoul of Boston.[4] In 1911 the new owners, Edward Beale McLean and Evelyn Walsh McLean, added a dining room with two floors of bedrooms above to the north side of the main house. The addition, designed by local architect Milton W. Stratton, repeated the exterior treatment of the original cottage.[5]

Briars Servants' House (Richard Cheek).

1. *Ellsworth American*, March 3, 1881; *Bar Harbor Record*, March 17, 1887.
2. Sears and Thomas Musgrave began construction of the Shore Path in August, 1881. *Bar Harbor Tourist*, August 13, 1881.
3. *Bar Harbor Record*, September 4, 1890.
4. *Ellsworth American*, October 5, 1898. The bowling alley was converted into a summer home in 1940 by Arthur McFarland, a local architect.
5. *Bar Harbor Record*, May 17, 1911. This addition is visible in a photograph of The Briars published in *Lost Bar Harbor* by G. W. Helfrich and Gladys O'Neil, Camden, 1982.

Edgemere, detail of land elevation, circa 1885 (Courtesy of James B. Vickery).

Edgemere, Thomas Musgrave Cottage

dgemere's completion received a newspaper notice in June, 1881.[1] With this cottage Emerson exploited the full decorative potential of shingling, as was observed by Arnold Brunner in 1884:

The entire wall surface of Edgemere is of shingles, which are in great vogue here. We find them square, rounded, painted and hollowed and they are laid out straight, irregularly, in wavy or zigzag lines. Every variation seems to have been tried. The effect is generally good, especially on broad surfaces, as the shingles give scale to the building and make a much more interesting wall than clapboards.[2]

This effect is evident in a photograph taken about 1885 centering on the round stair tower and entrance porch. Unlike Redwood, Edgemere had little of the Richard Norman Shaw-inspired Queen Anne style ornament. Instead there is an eclectic blend that was typical of the American Queen Anne style as it began to incorporate Colonial Revival motifs. It was, of course, the shingling that dominated the design, and the ornamental trim, such as the porch pediment decoration on the servants' wing, was used fairly sparingly to add definition where necessary. Brunner's sketch of the ocean facade shows the narrow gable end facing the water. This elevation had a one story porch and a two story square projection with a segmented arched porch and observation platform in which Colonial Revival style moldings seem to have predominated. Unfortunately, no description of the floor plans has survived.

In 1883 Thomas Musgrave made some alterations, apparently to the south side where an interior dining room chimney was moved to the exterior and incorporated into a bay window. The newspaper account only mentions the builder, John H. Hopkins.[3]

Musgrave was a wealthy New York banker, who built a second, rather odd looking cottage nearby in 1886 and called it Mare Vista. He later went bankrupt and ended his years in a mental hospital.

1. *Bar Harbor Tourist*, June 11, 1881.
2. *Building*, Vol. III, No. 1, October, 1884.
3. *Mt. Desert Herald*, April 19, 1883.

Edgemere, land elevation, circa 1885 (Maine Historic Preservation Commission).

Highbrook, elevation facing the ocean, circa 1890 (Courtesy of the Bar Harbor Historical Society).

Highbrook, Mary Leeds Cottage

HIGHBROOK ROAD

BAR HARBOR

1881

BURNED IN 1947

Mrs. James Leeds of Boston began construction of her cottage in the summer of 1881, which was unusual as building activity usually took place over the winter months.[1] The carriage path entrance to the house circled in front of the narrow gable end, while the long elevation with a veranda extending to the service wing faced the ocean. The exterior was shingled with what in 1881 was becoming the usual variety of patterns for Emerson. There was little in the design of the outside that was particularly distinctive in the way of ornamentation, except for the gable end porch with its railing cut in a chevron pattern.

The exterior disguised a floor plan with a few surprises. The first floor had an irregularly-shaped hall extending across the entrance façade facing the driveway. At one end is the staircase and at the other, overlooking the ocean, is an octagonal bay. Behind this room was a parlor, a dining room, and a downstairs bedroom. Six more bedrooms, including one in a gable end projecting over the entrance, comprised the second floor. Mary Leeds evidently required several guest chambers, but the room arrangements do not suggest entertainment on a grand scale. Mrs. Leeds made minor renovations to the house in 1898.[2] This probably included the addition of a bathroom to the second floor over the main entrance, which is evident in a postcard view from about 1910. A 1926 newspaper article records that a new owner, Mrs. A. M. Patterson, hired local architect Arthur McFarland to make renovations to the interior of the house and covert the stable to a garage.[3]

1. *Mt. Desert Herald*, July 24, 1881.
2. *Bar Harbor Record*, October 26, 1898.
3. *Bar Harbor Record*, March 11, 1926.

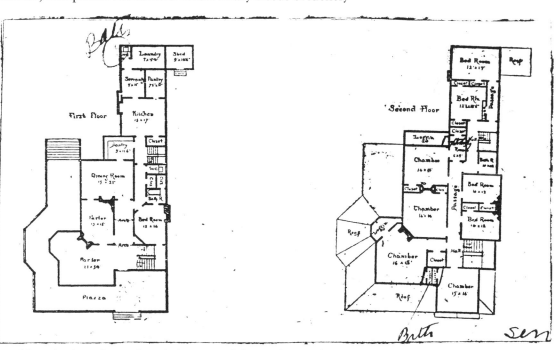

Highbrook, first floor plan (left), second floor plan (right) from real estate agent's rental book (Courtesy of Raymond L. Strout).

Thirlstane, perspective view by A.B. Johnson, *The Builder*, December 25, 1886 (Fine Arts Department, Boston Public Library, reproduced courtesy of the Trustees of the Boston Public Library).

Thirlstane, Mrs. R. B. Scott Cottage

BAR HARBOR

1881-82

BURNED IN 1947

Perhaps no other Shingle Style cottage is more often associated with Bar Harbor than Thirlstane, the cottage of Mrs. R. B. Scott of Washington, D. C. The reason for this is its dramatic ocean elevation, with its stair tower and observatory which, above the first story, was almost free-standing and strongly suggested a lighthouse. That we have a good representation of these features is due to the British journal, *The Builder*, which published a drawing by A. B. Johnson taken from a photograph. The comment that accompanied the illustration stated that, "This being a seaside villa, the architect seems to have had the rather happy idea of giving a kind of lighthouse effect to the prominent feature of the house, in keeping with the 'genius loci' ".[1] For the land side there are several photographs as well as sketches by John Calvin Stevens in 1883 and Arnold Brunner in 1884.[2]

The main section of Thirlstane was divided between the hall and parlor on one end and the library, dining room, and hallway at right angles adjoining the service wing. Typically, the living hall extended the width of the house and incorporated the stair tower. The hallway that led past the library between the living hall and the dining room served as more than simply a passageway. With two windows and a door, it acted as an additional room with a splendid view and also provided a transition between activities in the five main sections of the first floor: parlor, hall, library, dining room, and veranda. The second floor was logically laid out with each bedroom having a view. The only anomally was the bathroom in the bay over the porte cochere.[3] On the third floor was another large hall with access to a billiard room and the observation deck of the tower.

Arnold Brunner's sketch of the porte cochere was made with the following observations:

Rope curled in graceful spirals is used here and there for decoration. It is painted yellow on black or dark green ground, and is very effective, and moreover, furnishes us with a subject for debate—some of the party maintaining that it is "playful but proper", and others calling it "all wrong", and wondering what Ruskin would say about it.[4]

In 1888 Mrs. Scott hired a local contractor, Asa Hodgkins, to add a second story to the corner bay window in place of the balustrade. Notwithstanding this lady's long summer residence at Bar Harbor, little is known about her, which is unfortunate as Thirlstane's room arragements suggest that she led an active social life.[5]

Thirlstane, land side, circa 1885 (Maine Historic Preservation Commission).

Thirlstane, sketch by John Calvin Stevens dated September 3, 1883 (Courtesy of John Calvin Stevens II).

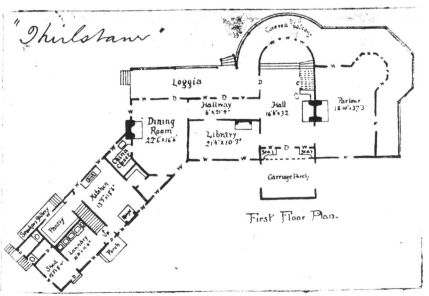

Thirlstane, first floor plan, from real estate agent's rental book (Courtesy of Raymond L. Strout).

A major remodeling of Thirlstane followed the purchase of the property by Colonel Edwin Morrill in 1898.[6] Colonel Morrill hired his fellow Philadelphians Cope and Stewardson to make extensive additions. A large library was added to the parlor on the east side and connected to the old room with sliding doors. The dining room was extended into the loggia, as was the hallway. In place of the old hallway, the former library was enlarged and became part of the hall. Also enlarged was the servants' wing, which received a two story addition. In making these changes Thirlstane was transformed from a modest summer cottage typical of the 1880s in Bar Harbor to a grand country residence suitable for large-scale entertainment and thus more typical of the resort during the 1890s.

1. *The Builder*, London, December 25, 1886.

2. *Stevens Sketch Book; Building*, Vol. III, No. 1, October, 1884. Raymond Strout has two rare photographs of the ocean side, but these postdate the 1898 additions.

3. The plans illustrated reflect Emerson's original scheme except for the second story bay window in the corner bedroom, which was added in 1888. The publication of these plans clarify the plan illustrated in Zaitzevsky which reflected the 1898 *remodeling*.

4. *Building, op. cit.*

5. *Mt. Desert Herald*, November 30, 1888.

6. *Bar Harbor Record*, March 30, 1898; November 16, 1898.

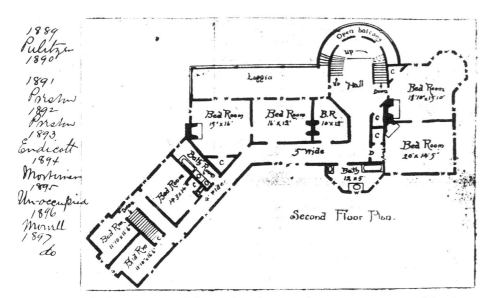

Thirlstane, second floor plan, from real estate agent's rental book (Courtesy of Raymond L. Strout).

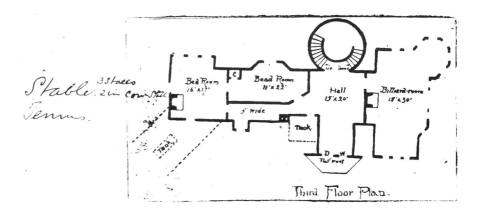

Thirlstane, third floor plan, from real estate agent's rental book (Courtesy of Raymond L. Strout).

Beau Desert, land elevation by William R. Emerson (Gerrish Collection, Jesup Memorial Library, Bar Harbor).

Beau Desert, land side, circa 1885 (Maine Historic Preservation Commission).

Beau Desert, Walter S. Gurnee Cottage

EDEN STREET

BAR HARBOR

1881-82

DESTROYED IN 1938

The construction of this cottage was first announced in September, 1881. A newspaper description of its "nearly completed" state followed in April, 1882. The clients, Mr. and Mrs. Walter Gurnee of New York, built one of the larger estates of its time. The house included a billiard room, a gymnasium, and numerous bedrooms. When President Benjamin Harrison visited Bar Harbor in 1889, the last party was a dinner and musical program at Beau Desert given by the Gurnees.[1] Beau Desert is the only Maine project by Emerson from the 1880s for which original drawings of the exterior survive. These consist of three elevations and two upper floor plans on linen. The lack of an original first floor plan must be supplemented by the 1882 newspaper description.

Although entirely shingled on the exterior, the design for Beau Desert included a Romanesque style porte cochere and tower and a porch with Moorish arches. Interestingly, both the tower and porte cochere were altered in execution to eliminate Romanesque motifs. In any case, these details were secondary to the overall effect. This cottage sprawled along the shore with extraordinarily varied fenestration and complex roof forms. Yet the house demonstrated Emerson's ability to incorporate a great many disparate elements into a cohesive composition.

A period newspaper description is helpful in conveying the grand scale of the interior:

The house may be entered on the lower floor by twelve different doors, and French windows open upon the front balcony. Cloisters are formed at either end and in the middle. At the south end, on the third floor, is a spacious billiard-room opening into a small room in the southeast tower. A hall extends from the side center of the billiard-room through the entire house, and at its end are the back stairs.[2]

Sixteen fireplaces, a gymnasium on the third floor, a cellar under the entire structure, and gas lighting were also part of the embellishments of this estate. There was also a stable and carriage house, for which no views have been located.

Thanks to Arnold Brunner's sketches, we have some sense of the interior design. There was a strong eclectic blend, as Brunner noted: "The walls are covered with a paper of a wave-like pattern, the color being varied in the different rooms, but the same design used throughout. The staircase at the end of the hall is original, and lattice-work and horseshoe arches give it a character a little surprising, perhaps, considering the very Colonial doorway." And he might have added the mantel in the hall with its boldly scaled broken pediment.[3]

Beau Desert, porch detail, sketch by Arnold W. Brunner, *Building*, December, 1884 (Fine Arts Department, Boston Public Library, reproduced courtesy of the Trustees of the Boston Public Library).

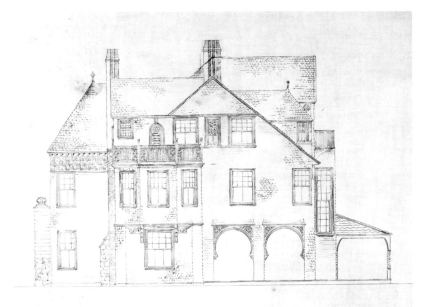

Beau Desert, end elevation by William R. Emerson (Gerrish Collection, Jesup Memorial Library, Bar Harbor).

Beau Desert, end elevation, circa 1885 (Maine Historic Preservation Commission).

Beau Desert, ocean elevation by William R. Emerson (Gerrish Collection, Jesup Memorial Library, Bar Harbor).

Emerson's drawings for Beau Desert survived in the office of the Bar Harbor architect Fred L. Savage, who made extensive renovations for the Gurnees' son Augustus in 1900-01. These included the enclosure of a portion of the porte cochere in glass, moving the entrance and staircase, and enlarging a balcony.[4] A. C. Gurnee's address was New York and Paris, and one can presume that his loyalty to Bar Harbor was not as consistent as his mother's, a long-time summer resident who died in 1925. The house was demolished in 1938, presumably for tax purposes.

1. *Mt. Desert Herald*, September 3, 1881; October 15, 1881; November 19, 1881; April 15, 1882; *Bar Harbor Record*, August 15, 1889.
2. *Mt. Desert Herald*, April 15, 1882.
3. *Building*, Vol. III, No. 3, December, 1884.
4. *Bar Harbor Record*, June 20, 1900.

Beau Desert, sketches of stairhall and hall mantel by Arnold W. Brunner, *Building*, December, 1884 (Fine Arts Department, Boston Public Library, reproduced courtesy of the Trustees of the Boston Public Library).

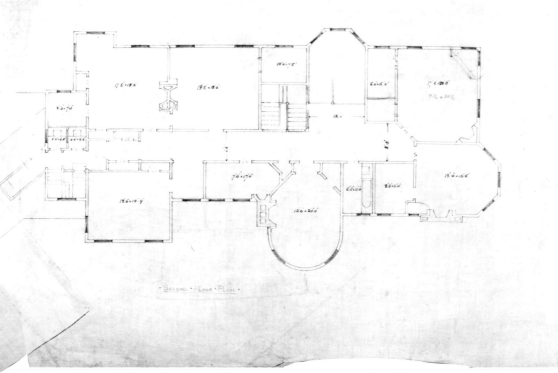

Beau Desert, second floor plan by William R. Emerson (Gerrish Collection, Jesup Memorial Library, Bar Harbor).

The Eyrie and The Craigs, Robert Amory Cottages, circa 1898 (Maine Historic Preservation Commission).

The Craigs and The Eyrie, Dr. Robert Amory Cottages

Dr. Robert Amory was one of the most loyal and dedicated summer residents. Throughout his life the Brookline, Massachusetts, physician remained involved in the affairs of his adopted community, even to the extent of making special visits to vote in town meetings. It is ironic that the first cottage Emerson designed for Dr. Amory will always be over-shadowed by the published design by Bruce Price which was not built. Evidently Dr. Amory first considered of a summer cottage at Bar Harbor in 1879, the year New York architect Bruce Price was working on the new West End Hotel. Price produced a design for a palatial estate which would have rivaled the grandest homes built in Bar Harbor during the 1890s and early 1900s. This highly picturesque scheme was published in the *American Architect and Building News* on December 27, 1879.

The project was too ambitious for Dr. Amory, who did not secure a building lot until December, 1880. By June, 1881, construction was nearly complete, and the *Bar Harbor Tourist* commented that, "We have no feeling of envy about us, but if we did, we don't think we could look at his cottage so often as we do, raised up to the highest point of Sugar Loaf Mountain and above the tall trees which spring from the hillside, so unique in architecture and so romantic in surroundings, without wishing to be in his place."[1]

This description seems to fit the Bruce Price scheme, but it applys to an Emerson design for which only one distant view has been located. This photograph of Amory Hill, taken about 1898, shows a rambling Shingle Style structure with a two story porch and a circular corner tower supporting a conical roof. The *Tourist* briefly described the interior, stating that it "has this novel feature in its inside finish; none of its walls are plastered, but instead, are shingled between the studing. The fire-places, shingles and general finish, in some rooms are spruce, in some ash, in the front rooms cedar. Besides this the walls of the parlor are dressed in pretty cambric and the seams covered with strips."[2]

Dr. Amory sold the cottage to his mother, Mary Amory, in 1882 and hired Emerson to design a second cottage called "The Eyrie". The doctor's heirs demolished The Craigs after World War II.

AMORY HILL
BAR HARBOR
1881-82
THE CRAIGS:
DESTROYED IN 1946
THE EYRIE:
BURNED IN 1899

The Eyrie, circa 1898 (Courtesy of the Bar Harbor Historical Society).

Dr. Amory's second Emerson cottage, built within a year of The Craigs, established a family compound on the small hill south of Mt. Desert Street. In selling The Craigs to his mother, Dr. Amory built a new Shingle Style residence nearer the south end of the hill.[3] This gave him a more prominent location, as is evident in a distant photograph (not pictured) taken from Kebo Street to the west. This view, which is in the archives of S.P.N.E.A., provides a general outline of the structure, whose treatment appeared quite simple. The one closer view of its east side shows that, except for a rather exotic bellcote dormer, much of the exterior ornament probably derived from varied shingle patterns.

In 1887 Dr. Amory made a two story addition to the house consisting of a kitchen and icehouse with servants' rooms above.[4] This was probably designed by Emerson, and the architect may have been involved in further changes made in 1899.[5] On September 7, 1899, a fire in a defective chimney resulted in the destruction of the house. A new residence was immediately built on the site by the contractors for the addition, Goddard & Hunt. This local firm of architect-builders and real estate brokers are credited with the design of the new Eyrie.[6] That building was demolished in 1942, and a new house built on the site in 1950.

1. *Bar Harbor Tourist*, June 15, 1881.
2. *Bar Harbor Tourist*, July 2, 1881.
3. *Mt. Desert Herald*, October 8, 1881; Hancock County Registry of Deeds.
4. *Mt. Desert Herald*, December 22, 1887.
5. *Bar Harbor Record*, February 8, 1899.
6. *Bar Harbor Record*, September 13, 1899; January 3, 1900. Paul Hunt was the son of William M. Hunt, the artist brother of architect Richard Morris Hunt. The photograph of The Eyrie which appears in *Lost Bar Harbor* is the 1900 structure by Goddard & Hunt. The same book identifies a photograph of The Craigs which I believe to be The Eyrie. That identification derived from a descendent of Dr. Amory. Nonetheless, I believe a circa 1898 view of the two cottages establishes that my identification of The Eyrie is correct.

Shore Acres, ocean side, *Inland Architect and News Record,* October, 1888 (Fine Arts Department, Boston Public Library, reproduced courtesy of the Trustees of the Boston Public Library).

Shore Acres, Dr. Hasket Derby Cottage

D r. Hasket Derby, a founder of the profession of ophthalmology in America, first erected a cottage on this site in 1869-70 at about the same time his fellow Bostonians Alpheus Hardy, George Minot, and F. M. Weld built on lots to the north of him. These men were among the first summer residents. In 1881 Dr. Derby replaced his smaller structure with a large cottage. As chairman of the building committee for St. Sylvia's Catholic Church, he would have become acquainted with Emerson. Construction of Shore Acres was announced in the local newspaper in December, 1881, and by April the house was nearly completed.[1]

The Derby Cottage was different from many of the early Bar Harbor cottages in having two formal elevations. This may have been due to its location on a semi-public lot fronting the Shore Path and near the center of the village. The central section of the ocean elevation featured a steep hipped roof with ornamental chimneys flanking a balustrade. The effect was more suggestive of a Georgian manor than the vernacular structures that normally served as inspiration for Emerson. This Georgian influence was also reflected in the floor plan, which consisted of a central hall flanked by a dining room on one side and a library and a parlor on the other.

The Georgian influence can easily be over-stated, however, for the house appears to have had a rather complex floor plan. A photograph taken from the southwest provides a perspective that enables one to appreciate the difficulty in analyzing this design without architectural plans. According to an 1882 account, an interesting feature was the main staircase: "The stairs in the main hall are of three or five steps to a section, the sections at right angles with each other, and on the second landing is a bridge spanning a space between two halls." This description sounds very similar to the staircase in the Sanford House at Newport, Rhode Island, of 1869-70 by Emerson & Fehmer.[2]

Shore Acres, ocean side, circa 1890 (Courtesy of Raymond L. Strout).

Shore Acres, land side, circa 1890 (Courtesy of Raymond L. Strout).

Another unusual detail of the Derby Cottage was the porch posts, which were shingled in a banded effect and supported Colonial Revival style arched openings. This banding was also employed on St. Sylvia's Church.

Dr. Derby hired Emerson again to design a house for him in Boston in 1885-86. That formal and elegant Colonial Revival design is comparable to the work of his more academically-oriented contemporaries, such as McKim, Mead & White.

1. *Mt. Desert Herald*, December 10, 1881; April 8, 1882.
2. *Mt. Desert Herald*, April 8, 1882. For a photograph of the staircase in the Sanford House, see Zaitzevsky, *op. cit.*, Plate 2.

Cottages in The Field, Bar Harbor, circa 1890. Side view of Shore Acres showing the rear of the service wing (Courtesy of the Archives, Society for the Preservation of New England Antiquities).

Mossley Hall, east elevation, circa 1885 (Maine Historic Preservation Commission).

Mossley Hall, William B. Howard Cottage

HIGHBROOK ROAD

BAR HARBOR

1882-83

DESTROYED CIRCA 1945

Few of Emerson's summer cottages have excited as much interest among architectural historians as Mossley Hall. According to a Bar Harbor newspaper, the architect was given "carte blanche" to design this extraordinary summer residence.[1] The client, William B. Howard, was a Chicago builder known for the construction of the Indiana State House, the New York Aquaduct, and the Nickel Plate Railroad. Howard and his family visited Bar Harbor in the summer of 1881 and evidently made the decision to build in the following year. Construction was announced in November, 1882, and the house was nearing completion in April, 1883, when the local reporter gained access for inspection.[2] So notable was Mossley Hall that it was included by George Sheldon in his prestigious publication *Artistic County Seats* of 1886.[3]

The name of the house, which is so unlike most of the other summer cottages, probably derives from "Moseley Old Hall", a country estate in England.[4] It is, therefore, probably no accident that this cottage is one of the few that bears similarities to the country homes of the English aristocracy. A comparison with the early work of Richard Norman Shaw, such as Cragside in Northumberland (begun in 1870), illustrates how Mossley Hall corresponds to the sprawling picturesque estates of that great British architect. While there is nothing specifically derivative from the work of Shaw, or any other architect, the massing of Mossley Hall with its complex multi-faceted elevations is characteristic (albeit on a much smaller scale) of country estates in Britain.

If there was a principal elevation for this house, it was the east side with its twin gable end projecting from a long rectangular facade. This boldly articulated gable end had a broad two story bay window that contained the parlor which, opening into the hall behind it, formed a grandly spacious room with views looking out to sea.

Mossley Hall, northeast view, circa 1900 (Courtesy of the Bar Harbor Historical Society).

Mossley Hall, view from southeast, circa 1885, from Sheldon's *Artistic Country Seats*, reprinted as *American Country Houses of the Gilded Age* (Courtesy of Dover Publications, Inc.).

Geometric exterior ornament, including shingles applied in a manner to resemble Romanesque brick diapering, provided the dominant decorative motifs.

To the right of the central gable end was a porch off the parlor, which in turn was connected by an open veranda around the north gable end that contained the study, a room with its own private exterior entrance. To the left of the east gable end was a carriage pass-through under a wing joined to a tower containing the billiard hall and observation platform. The striking pattern of open grid-work in the gable end was scaled to provide a balance to the strong design features of the main section of the house. Symbolically, its semi-detached position emphasized its function as primarily a male refuge.

No less visually dramatic was the south elevation, in which the firmly grounded east facade seemed to give way to those sections of the house that appeared to cascade down the hill. The restless character of this facade was counter-balanced at the end of the servants' wing by a small porch designed in the form of a buttress, which was also mirrored in the raking gable end of that wing. This side of the house contained the main entrance hidden under the

Mossley Hall, detail of tower staircase by Arnold W. Brunner, *Building*, December, 1884. (Fine Arts Department, Boston Public Library, reproduced courtesy of the Trustees of the Boston Public Library).

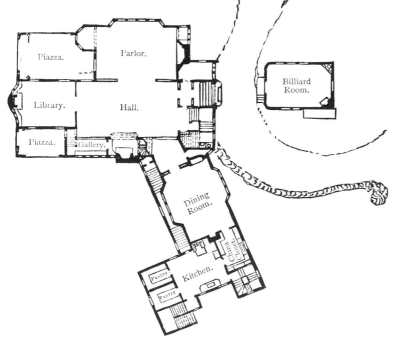

Mossley Hall, first floor plan from Sheldon's *Artistic Country Seats*, reprinted as *American Country Houses of the Gilded Age* (Courtesy of Dover Publications, Inc.). East side at top of plan.

Mossley Hall, southeast view, circa 1885 (Maine Historic Preservation Commission).

Mossley Hall, southwest view, circa 1885 (Maine Historic Preservation Commission).

carriage pass-through. More prominent was the massive multi-paned window which lighted the staircase in the hall. The hall was, of course, the central room of the house and contained the traditional fireplace inglenook, as well as a picture gallery behind a platform railing to the right. The gallery, a very English feature, could also have been viewed from the second floor above. According to Arnold Brunner, whose sketches provide the only illustrations of the interior, the fireplace inglenook was sufficiently recessed to contain a room above, accessed via a winding staircase, with two windows opening onto the parlor.[5] To the left of the staircase window was the dining room, positioned between the hall and the servants' wing. A large bay window afforded a view of the mountains.

Arnold Brunner also provided the only representation available of the stable for Mossley Hall. His sketch is supplemented with the following comments: "Mr. Howard's stable is as clever a building in its way as his house. Its

Mossley Hall, sketch of staircase by Arnold W. Brunner, *Building,* December, 1884.

Mossley Hall Carriage Barn, sketch by Arnold W. Brunner, *Building,* December, 1884 (Fine Arts Department, Boston Public Library, reproduced courtesy of the Trustees of the Boston Public Library).

Mossley Hall, southwest view showing dining room and staircase bays, circa 1885 (Maine Historic Preservation Commission).

double gable is partly supported by shingled brackets, one on each side of the little bay which seems to grow out of the front wall."[6]

William B. Howard died in 1898, and the family continued to own the property until 1909, when it was "thoroughly renovated" for rental use.[7] It then began a long decline in use that reflected Bar Harbor's history as a resort for the very wealthy. Had the house not been demolished, it would have fallen victim to the 1947 fire.

1. *Industrial Journal*, Bangor, November 10, 1882.
2. *Bar Harbor Tourist*, August 13, 1881; *Mt. Desert Herald*, November 2, 1882; April 12, 1883. The latter newspaper description contains the only record of the rooms on the upper floors.
3. George W. Sheldon, *Artistic County-Seats: Types of Recent American Villa and Cottage Architecture with Instances of Country Club-Houses*, New York, 1886-87, Plate 51.
4. There is no similarity in appearance between the two houses.
5. *Building*, Vol. III, No. 3, December, 1884.
6. *Ibid.*
7. *Bar Harbor Record*, May 19, 1909.

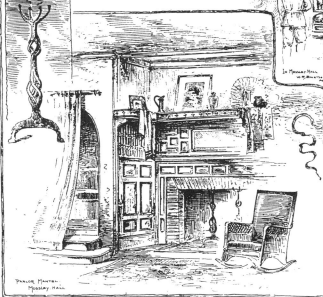

Mossley Hall, sketches of fireplace inglenooks by Arnold W. Brunner, *Building*, December, 1884 (Fine Arts Department, Boston Public Library, reproduced courtesy of the Trustees of the Boston Public Library).

Unidentified Cottage

n 1886 a French publication, *L'Architecture Americaine*, featured two photographic plates of a "vestibule" in a summer residence at Northeast Harbor by William R. Emerson.[1] An extensive building survey of the town conducted in 1985 failed to identify any cottage, including those no longer standing, which might have contained this room. The photographs of this room are important in that they record what can be considered as representative of the architect's concepts of interior design for summer cottages during the early 1880s.

An interesting feature of this room (which should more properly be called a "hall" rather than a "vestibule") was the use of wood shingles. These formed the wainscot, with a saw-tooth pattern suggesting a chair rail, and also encased the exposed studs above. Between these studs the walls were decorated with what appears to have been an ornamental embossed leather. The frieze that separated the vestibule from the stairhall contained four panels, each with its own delicate pattern. From what is known about Emerson's work, it is probable that he designed every detail of the interior, including the fireplace andirons and the brackets supporting the mantelshelf.

1. *L'Architecture Americaine*, reprinted as *American Victorian Architecture*, New York, 1975, Plates 31 and 32.

Two views of the vestibule, cottage at Northeast Harbor, circa 1885, reprinted in *American Victorian Architecture*, 1975 (Courtesy of Dover Publications, Inc.).

Homewood, circa 1890 (Courtesy of Raymond L. Strout).

Homewood, Mrs. M. D. Sanders Cottage

Homewood was a distinctive small cottage which probably owed its unusual configuration to its steep wooded site. By 1883 lots with views were expensive in Bar Harbor, and Mrs. Sanders, who was from Philadelphia, hired Emerson to make the most of an awkward location.[1] The floor plans reveal that the cottage was terraced with the "basement" level projecting out from the main block of the house and thereby also serving as a floor for the veranda above. With a siting so that the front faced northeast and the side faced southeast, a maximum exposure was obtained for a hillside lot. The exterior detailing was quite simple, the only embellishments being oval windows in the forward gable ends.

Presumably, the real estate broker's floor plans are an accurate representation of the original scheme. They show the traditional arrangement in which the parlor and dining room received the most light, while the sitting room occupied the more private location.[2]

EAGLE LAKE ROAD

BAR HARBOR

1883

BURNED IN 1947

1. In 1887, when Mrs. Sanders built a second cottage, "Pinehurst", on an adjoining lot, she simply hired a local builder. Bar Harbor had reached the peak of its speculative boom by that time.

2. The citation that Emerson designed this cottage can be found in a list of cottages and their architects in the *Bar Harbor Record*, March 17, 1887.

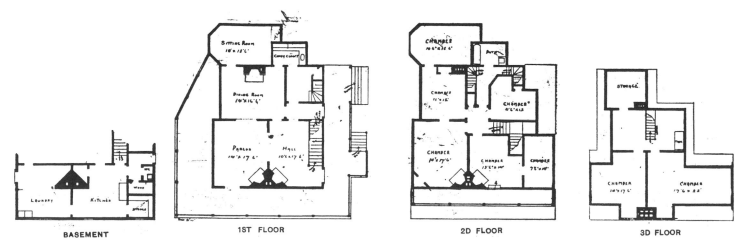

Homewood, four floor plans from real estate agent's rental book (Courtesy of Raymond L. Strout).

Sproul's Market

Henry C. Sproul's new market created considerable comment in the *Mt. Desert Herald* for a commercial building. The long description of the building which appeared in May, 1883, followed notices of the progress of construction in January and April.[1] Typical was the observation that "the elegant paneled front of Mr. H. C. Sproul's new market will be an ornament to the street".[2] This is not surprising, given the vernacular character of contractor-built commercial blocks in Bar Harbor at the time, which is evident in the only known photograph that includes the Emerson building. Sproul's Market was an extremely rare example of the architect's scheme for a wooden commercial structure.

The principal elevation featured an elaborate Colonial Revival style facade. The entablature included paneling, corner consoles, and a broken pediment. The balustrade above was comprised of a central panel containing an oval with radiating louvers. According to the newspaper, this facade was painted in dark green and yellow.

Although long-since demolished, Sproul's Market was part of a tradition of fancifully designed commercial buildings which has recently re-emerged in Bar Harbor.

1. *Mt. Desert Herald*, May 10, 1883; January 1, 1883; January 25, 1883; April 19, 1883.
2. *Mt. Desert Herald*, January 11, 1883.

Sproul's Market, advertisement from *Mt. Desert Herald*, 1883 (Bar Harbor Historical Society).

Main Street, Bar Harbor, Sproul's Market fifth from left, circa 1890 (Courtesy of the Archives, Society for the Preservation of New England Antiquities).

St. Peter's Episcopal Church

9 WHITE STREET

ROCKLAND

1883-84

Shingle Style architecture is commonly associated with wooded coastal sites, where it is accepted that a part of the objective will be for the building to blend with its natural surroundings. This was not the case, however, with Rockland's St. Peter's Episcopal Church which stands now, as it did in 1884, in a densely built urban neighborhood surrounded by residences and the Knox County Courthouse. Construction began in October, 1883, and was substantially completed by June of the following year. The original church had a seating capacity of 150 and was evidently designed with no wasted space. There was a small room for organ and choir, a rector's room, and a sanctuary which featured a pulpit "finished with miniature hard pine shingles". The cost of the building came to $2,000.[1]

Certainly a congregation in a community the size of Rockland would have anticipated that the church would require additional space. Indeed, that is what happened, and it is why the only views we have of the original building are two sketches made shortly after its completion. The first one is by Arnold Brunner, who stopped in Rockland on his way to sketch architecture at Bar Harbor in 1884.[2] The second appeared in *The Century Magazine* in January, 1885, and appears to have been rendered by Emerson himself.[3] A comparison is interesting, for whereas Brunner saw a

St. Peter's Episcopal Church, perspective view by William R. Emerson,
The Century Magazine, January, 1885
(Courtesy of Earle G. Shettleworth, Jr.).

Sketch of St. Peter's Church by Arnold W. Brunner, *Building*, October, 1884 (Fine Arts Department, Boston Public Library, reproduced courtesy of the Trustees of the Boston Public Library).

Shingle Style church, Emerson clearly intended something closer to an English Cotswold cottage. The Emerson view shows wood shingles thickly laid to suggest a thatch roof, heavy paneled doors, and a brick chimney with decorative chimney pots. Which interpretation was closer to reality is difficult to determine as the only section of the original church that is still visible, the west gable end and entry porch, has roofing shingles that are asphalt.

Major additions to the church began in 1890-91. The long 22 x 40 foot nave added to the south front of the building was designed in a compatible Shingle Style by Edward F. Glover, architect for the local contracting firm of William H. Glover and Company.[4] This extension included a full basement, which required that the ridge of the new roof rise above that of the original building. Both the nave and the basement had their own entrances, each with a shingled portico patterned after the ones by Emerson. Also, a choir room was added under the west end below the belfry.

Other changes followed a fire on November 24, 1901. In 1902 the south entrance was rebuilt in a graceful, serpentine fashion, which has subsequently been straightened again. In 1931 the nave was extended out of the north side of the original building. More recently, a parish hall built on the east side included a one story connector that obscures most of Emerson's 1884 gable end and entry on that side.

St. Peter's Church,
circa 1905
(Maine Historic
Preservation Commission).

St. Peter's Episcopal Church, Rockland Me

Handcolored

1. *Courier-Gazette*, Rockland, September 2, 1884; July 28, 1891.
2. *The Builder*, Vol. III, No. 1, October, 1884.
3. Maria G. van Rensselaer, "Churches", *The Century Magazine*, Vol. XXIX, January, 1885, p. 334.
4. *Courier-Gazette*, Rockland, November 24, 1891. The Glover firm was the original contractor for the church.

Brookend, Samuel E. Lyons Cottage

DUCK BROOK

BAR HARBOR

1884

BURNED CIRCA 1963

S amuel Lyons, a wealthy New York lawyer, acquired a large parcel of land in the Duck Brook vicinity north of the village in 1869. Over the years he built four cottages in 1869, 1880-81, 1884, and 1886. Except for the latter, which was sold before completion and burned one month later, these cottages were apparently mostly for family use, including his daughter and son-in-law, General William F. Smith. The documentation is not clear, but apparently Lyons built "Shore Acres" in 1869, then "Edenfield" for the Smiths in 1880-81 (see Part Two), and finally Brookend. Construction on the latter began at the end of August, 1884, and the house stood finished in January, 1885.[1] Lyons died in 1887, and in 1888 this became the Smiths' summer home until they sold it to Dr. Robert Abbe in 1898.

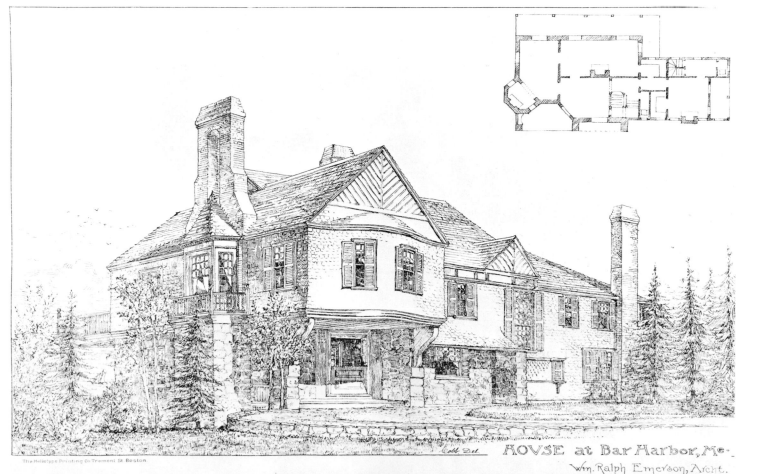

Brookend, perspective view by Albert Winslow Cobb, *American Architect and Building News,* June 28, 1884 (Courtesy of Earle G. Shettleworth, Jr.).

Brookend, land side,
circa 1895,
(Courtesy of
the Bar Harbor
Historical Society).

The best view of Brookend is Albert Winslow Cobb's rendering which appeared in the *American Architect and Building News* on June 28, 1884, as "House at Bar Harbor". Brookend differed from much of the architect's work in Maine in that it was more suggestive of a small suburban dwelling than a picturesque summer home. In fact, the house hardly can be considered Shingle Style and owes more to the English Queen Anne style as loosely interpreted by American architects. Certainly there were many features which departed from the predominant characteristics of Emerson's work throughout the 1880s.[2] The first story of the main section of the house was fieldstone with the bowfronted gable end projecting over the entrance porch. The Queen Anne style half-timbering in the pediments on the principal elevation can be found on other Emerson projects, but rarely by this time as such a prominent decorative motif.

The floor plan was exceptionally good for a house of this size. The three principal rooms, the hall, parlor, and dining room, were neatly arranged into almost three equal sections with convenient circulation. The hall, entered through a Dutch door off the sheltered entrance porch, provided logical access to the other rooms. On the north end was the parlor with its inglenook built into the corner chimney. On the second floor were bedrooms arranged off a central hall.[3]

The only photographs of the ocean side were taken after additions in 1900. Apparently this elevation consisted of a large gable end identical to the land side but flanked by twin dormers. A one story veranda extended across this facade and was supported on a stone wall at the very edge of the shore.

In 1899 Dr. Abbe hired Ecole des Beaux Arts-trained New York architect Edwin Denby to extensively enlarge and remodel Brookend. A 144 foot wing added to the north side at least doubled the size of the house. At the same time the main entrance was moved to the window next to the staircase and the hall enlarged into the old dining room. The windows on the water side were enlarged with bay windows on the second story. Finally, a porte cochere was added.[4] Thus, Emerson's modest cottage became a grand Bar Harbor summer home.

1. *Mt. Desert Herald*, August 22, 1884; January 30, 1885. The progress of construction was noted in issues of September 19, 1884; November 7, 1884; and November 21, 1884.
2. One wonders what contribution Cobb may have made to this design as well as to that of Bournemouth a year later.

3. Raymond Strout's rental property record book includes both floor plans.
4. *Bar Harbor Record*, January 24, 1900.

The Knoll, Miss H. C. Wilkins Cottage

Miss Wilkins purchased a small lot next to Mrs. Sanders, who had hired Emerson to design Homewood Cottage in 1883. The two Philadelphia women were evidently related, and they obtained similar designs adapted to the rugged terrain of their property. Construction on The Knoll was announced in November, 1884, and plastering of the interior was underway in March, 1885.[1] Emerson's design was a variation on Homewood Cottage and repeated the earlier solution for a steep site by creating a terraced effect in the plan. With The Knoll, the second and third floors consisted of twin gable roofs that were apparently separated into two sections to obtain more natural light for the uphill exposures. Such a novel arrangement made this cottage a particularly interesting solution for the problem of an inexpensive house on a difficult site.

1. *Mt. Desert Herald*, November 7, 1884; March 2, 1885. Emerson is identified as the architect in a list of cottages and their architects that appeared in the *Bar Harbor Record*, March 17, 1887.

EAGLE LAKE ROAD
BAR HARBOR
1884-85
BURNED IN 1947

The Knoll, circa 1890 (Courtesy of Raymond L. Strout).

Mt. Desert Reading Room, circa 1910 (Courtesy of the Archives, Society for the Preservation of New England Antiquities).

Mt. Desert Reading Room

Founded in 1881, the Mt. Desert Reading Room was established to "promote literacy and social culture".[1] It also served as a club where alcohol could be served in a state where prohibition was in effect in the nineteenth century. The club acquired the Veazie Cottage near this site, which was remodeled in 1881.[2] By 1885 the needs of the group were such that Emerson was hired to develop plans for a 30 x 70 foot two story addition to include a music hall.[3] Over the next year the decision was made to build a new structure instead, moving the Veazie Cottage to another site. By September, 1886, Emerson had the plans ready for construction.[4]

The large clubhouse that was completed by the summer of 1887 is domestic in scale and materials. Yet its vertical proportions, square shape, and lack of a service wing immediately distinguish it from the summer cottages. Although shingled, Colonial Revival style details predominate. The hipped roof is quite steep, and there are pedimented dormers and gable ends as well as sash with twelve-over-twelve lights. On the roof was a look-out with a railing in a Chippendale pattern.

All of this, however, was subordinated to the most distinctive features: the porch and bow window on the principal facade. The porch, which rests on a tall granite foundation, extends around the sides of the clubhouse, curving around the bow window at the northeast corner. The porch posts were tapered at the bottom, suggesting the "gun-stock" corner posts found in eighteenth century construction. These posts were more than an archaeological curiosity, for they added

Mt. Desert Reading Room, east elevation, circa 1910 (Maine Historic Preservation Commission).

Mt. Desert Reading Room, circa 1900 (Courtesy of the Bar Harbor Historical Society).

visual emphasis to the support of the porch and the elliptical arch, particularly as they were widely spaced. Using simple materials and spare detailing, Emerson created a powerful composition which commanded a highly distinctive presence in the harbor.

The interior was described in the *Mt. Desert Herald*, but no plans or views have come to light.[5] The Mt. Desert Reading Room lasted until 1922, when changes in Bar Harbor's social life brought its demise. Other gathering places, such as cottages, yachts, and specialized clubs offered more freedom for social interaction. The Maine Central Railroad purchased the building and adjoining pier in 1924, leasing it to the Bar Harbor Yacht Club. That organization was dissolved in 1932, and the clubhouse was taken over by the Shore Club. Between 1948 and 1950 the building was converted into the Bar Harbor Hotel, and a large modern wing was added to the rear.[6] At that time the interior lost most of its original features.

The additions and interior conversions were in some ways not as detrimental as changes to the principal elevation. The gun-stock porch posts and elliptical arch were removed when the semi-circular portion of the porch was glazed to become the hotel dining room. The conical roof on the bow window was replaced with one having a barely perceptible pitch, and the design of the roof railings was simplified. These features were critical to the character of original design and probably could have been incorporated into the remodeling.

1. *Bar Harbor Tourist*, August 3, 1881.
2. *Bar Harbor Tourist*, June 15, 1881. Actually the Veazie Cottage had been acquired by an earlier organization, the Oasis Club, which merged with the new group.
3. *Mt. Desert Herald*, September 11, 1885.
4. *Mt. Desert Herald*, September 24, 1886.
5. *Mt. Desert Herald*, May 6, 1887.
6. *Lost Bar Harbor, op. cit.*, pp. 116-117.

Bournewood, circa 1890, with first floor plan, bottom left, and second floor plan, bottom right (Courtesy of Raymond L. Strout).

Bournemouth, W. B. Walley Cottage

EDEN STREET

BAR HARBOR

1885-86

DESTROYED IN 1979

Bournemouth shared with Brookend a rather formal, suburban character with just the basic number of rooms required for a summer cottage on a prime lot in Bar Harbor. W. B. Walley, a Boston lawyer, began construction in September, 1885, and the house was completed in time for the 1886 season.[1] The first story was of stone, while the upper floors of wood projected into a five-and-a-half foot overhang. Although asymmetrical, there was a neat, ordered appearance produced by the land facade. In a kind of mock-Tudor, the shingled second story was embellished with wood posts suggesting the studs of a balloon frame rather than heavy timber framing.

To the right of the main entrance the wall bowed outward to reflect a semi-circular staircase. In an unusually efficient use of space, this stairway was located off both the hall and the dining room, being separated from the latter by sliding doors. Like Brookend, these stairs led to a central hallway on the second floor with bedrooms on all sides. As with many summer cottages, the library formed a separate sanctuary with its own exterior entrance. This was especially pronounced with Bournemouth, where it consisted of a one story wing separated from the parlor by a small hallway. The kitchen was located in the basement. Much of this plan can be "read" from the exterior: the T-shaped center section with the parlor in the gable end and the hall extending perpendicular to that, the staircase with its bowed front, and the library in a separate wing on the north side.

No views of the ocean side have been located, but the plans show a very generous space alloted for the piazza. The *Mt. Desert Herald* provided the following description: "On this side there are three bay windows, one large dormer window with a smaller one on each side. A piazza twenty-six feet wide runs almost the entire length of this side, in the center of which is a loggia 26 by 21 feet connected directly with the dining room, hall and parlor, and with the 'den' [library] by the piazza".

In 1926 a new owner of Bournemouth, Mrs. Robert Hall McCormick of Chicago, hired local architect Arthur McFarland to make extensive changes. The long piazza was replaced by a small recessed porch on the ocean side, and there was interior remodeling as well. A terrace was added off the parlor, which was probably part of the landscaping of the grounds designed by Beatrix Farrand.[2]

1. *Mt. Desert Herald*, September 11, 1885; March 19, 1886.
2. *Bar Harbor Transcript*, March 10, 1926.

Dr. A. H. Mason Cottage

AMORY HILL

BAR HARBOR

1887

BURNED IN 1907

This was the third shingled cottage Emerson designed on the small hill owned largely by Dr. Robert Amory. It is not clear if Dr. Amory or Dr. Mason commissioned this house, although it was known as the Mason Cottage. Dr. Mason was not a frequent summer visitor, and the house quickly became Dr. Amory's rental property. In 1907 it was partially burned in a fire and demolished.

No photographs have been located of this structure, but measured floor plans from a real estate agent's rental book can be considered an accurate representation of Emerson's plans.[1] The *Bar harbor Record* contained only this brief reference to the construction of the house: "W. F. Vose is putting the finishing touches on the painting of the Mason Cottage on Amory's Hill. The cottage is beautifully situated, commanding a fine view of the village and bay. The rooms are large and elegant and are finished in good taste. A laundry building which is separate from the main house, is conveniently fitted up for work. Isaac N. Mitchell is laying out the grounds around the cottage in a very tasteful and elegant manner".[2]

The narrow lot where the building was situated accounts for the rectangular plan, which was quite unremarkable in most respects. There was a covered piazza overlooking the ocean and a triangular bay window oriented to provide a vista from the center of the library, past the porch, toward the sea. A partition on the exterior staircase gave that room a private entrance as well.

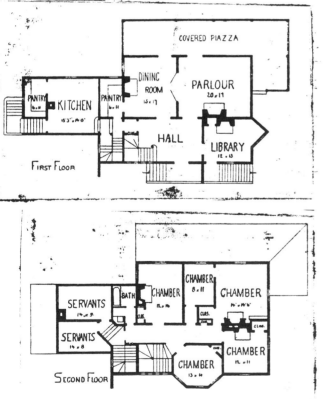

1. The citation that Emerson designed this cottage is a list of cottages and their architects that appeared in the *Bar Harbor Record* of March 17, 1887.
2. *Bar Harbor Record*, May 19, 1887.

Mason Cottage, first and second floor plans from real estate agent's rental book (Courtesy of Raymond L. Strout).

Fair Haven, Samuel H. Jones Cottage

The development of Cape Arundel as a summer resort for the wealthy began in the late 1880s. Samuel Jones, a Philadelphia millionaire and yachtsman, was one of the first to build a large architect-designed cottage on Ocean Avenue overlooking the Atlantic.[1] The Cape Arundel cottages generally differed from their Bar Harbor counterparts in that they were densely concentrated on small lots. Absent were the long service wings and landscaped grounds with serpentine carriage paths. A relatively small lot may account for the pronounced vertical proportions of Fair Haven. Construction occurred over the winter of 1887-88.[2]

The picturesque features of this cottage were quite striking. Viewed from the south, the dominant form was a large gambrel roof, while from the north it was a gable roof with wide overhanging eaves. This dichotomy was not apparent from either side due to the polygonal corner tower on one side and the use of a shingled "skirt" suggesting

Fair Haven, northeast view, circa 1895 (Reproduced by permission of the Kennebunkport Historical Society).

Fair Haven, southeast view with Samuel Jones in the foreground, circa 1895 (Reproduced by permission of the Kennebunkport Historical Society).

the gambrel form on the north end. The latter was a feature Emerson frequently employed with more subtlety in other projects. The wisteria-like vines that enveloped the porch in early photographs seem to have anchored the house to its site. Even without the vines, the porch, shingled and arcaded with round arches, provided a source of visual stability to the design, especially with its highly picturesque roof treatment.

A group of photographs owned by the Kennebunkport Historical Society documents the interior finishes. The walls in the hall appeared to have been similar to the unidentified house by Emerson in Northeast Harbor. In both cases shingled wainscot and studs were set off by a decorative material between the studs. The remainder of the ground floor received a variety of paneling treatments, and the fireplace mantels were almost austere in their simplicity. The light finish apparent on the woodwork is borne out in the following newspaper description: "Adjoining the large room is an octagonal tea room, in pure white, with white corduroy cushions and trimmings". There was also a ship's bunk with a port hole in the living room, as the dominant decorative motif was the interior of a yacht.[3]

Sometime before 1922 an enlargement of the service wing was made to the Jones Cottage. Fairhaven was torn down in 1971 to make way for a new residence.

1. Research by Kim Lovejoy, dated 1979, on file at the Maine Historic Preservation Commission, Augusta.
2. *Eastern Star*, Kennebunk, December 28, 1887.
3. *The Wave*, Kennebunkport, August 12, 1891.

Fair Haven, dining room, circa 1895 (Reproduced by permission of the Kennebunkport Historical Society).

Jayne Cottage, land side, circa 1890 (Courtesy of Raymond L. Strout).

Dr. Horace Jayne Cottage

Educated in Germany, the author of several books and member of the faculty of the University of Pennsylvania, Dr. Jayne was married to Caroline Furness, an author and niece of Philadelphia architect Frank Furness.[1] The Jaynes commissioned Emerson to build a cottage during the peak of Bar Harbor's development boom of the 1880s. Construction began in October, 1887, and by March, 1888, the house was being plastered.[2] Located in the hills near Mossley Hall, the Jayne Cottage was prominently sited above Bar Harbor. A view of the town from the east shows the outline of the structure with its gambrel roof end and long veranda.[3]

The main section of the house was 46 x 33 feet and the ell 44 x 25. As with several Bar Harbor cottages, locating the dining room in the wing accounted for the almost equal proportions of both sections.[4] The only photograph of the land side shows the house to have been entirely shingled with a circular entrance porch and a round arched Colonial Revival style stairhall window. This view, although showing only the mid-section of the house, reveals characteristics of Emerson's detailing. Each floor level was defined by delicately fabricated saw-tooth shingles that projected in a shallow overhang. Also visible in the photograph are a variety of unusual stained glass windows.

1. Although Dr. Jayne and his wife hired Emerson in Bar Harbor, this did not necessarily reflect an aversion to the work of Frank Furness, who designed the doctor's Philadelphia residence in 1895.
2. *Mt. Desert Herald*, October 14, 1887; March 30, 1888; *Bar Harbor Record*, March 22, 1888.
3. Photograph in the Archives of the Society for the Preservation of New England Antiquities, Boston.
4. *Bar Harbor Record*, March 22, 1888.

CLEFSTONE ROAD

BAR HARBOR

1887-88

BURNED IN 1947

Rock Ledge, circa 1895 (Courtesy of the Brick Store Museum, Kennebunk).

Rock Ledge (Richard Cheek).

Rock Ledge, E. Dunbar Lockwood Cottage

Rock Ledge succeeds where Fair Haven does not in illustrating Emerson's innovative use of the gambrel roof. With his own house in Milton in 1886, the architect created a long, rambling three story structure in which the gambrel is employed in a manner that blurred the distinctions between wall and roof. For Rock Ledge this formula is explored further by bringing the roof pitch down to the veranda that encircles three sides of the cottage. On both side elevations the second story windows are recessed behind the sloping plane of the gambrel and are flanked by skirting. The importance of the skirting is especially evident in the principal facade, which consists of the broad gable end of the gambrel. What could have been a static facade is enlivened by a triangular bay window supporting a third story balcony for a recessed porch. The delicate grid pattern of the balustrade and the heavily molded cornice supporting it give added definition to a house that is otherwise almost lacking in exterior moldings. Emerson's sense of subtle detail is also evident in the cantilevered staircase supported on scalloped brackets that are an extension of the porch siding. The parlor ceiling has a grid pattern which mirrors the design of the balcony railing.

Plans for Lockwood's cottage were prepared in late 1887, and the house was completed in 1888.[1] Like Samuel Jones who built Fair Haven, Dunbar Lockwood was from Philadelphia. The Lockwood Cottage survives largely intact but, where small details count so much in Emerson's work, alterations significantly detract from the original design. An enlargement of the ell spoils the crisp lines of the gambrel roof. Changes in the fenestration are also present, but are less visually detracting than the removal of the Ocean Avenue staircase and the increase in vegetation which obscures the base of the veranda.

1. *Eastern Star*, Kennebunk, December 28, 1887. A brief description of the cottage appears in *The Wave*, Kennebunkport, August 12, 1891.

Rock Ledge, parlor, circa 1895 (Courtesy of Suzanne and John Prunier).

St. Jude's Episcopal Church

The small summer colony at Seal Harbor organized an Episcopal congregation of its own in order not to have to travel to Bar Harbor or Northeast Harbor, the two closest communities. Both of those resorts began with small Episcopal churches that were quickly replaced or enlarged as their memberships expanded. Seal Harbor never outgrew the first structure. The mission in Seal Harbor was organized in November, 1886, with services held in a schoolhouse. Rufus R. Thomas of Philadelphia donated land, $600, and the cost of architectural plans.[1]

St. Jude's Episcopal Church, interior (Richard Cheek).

Work began in 1887; and although the church was opened that July, it was not finished until June, 1889, and consecrated in September. Delays were due to the lack of contributions from the small congregation.[2] The building has survived intact except for a modest guild house and winter chapel added to one corner in 1931.

St. Jude's is even smaller than the original St. Peter's in Rockland. In fact, the church originally consisted of nothing more than a nave enclosed by a gable roof with a combined entrance porch and belfry. The exterior is entirely shingled, including the buttresses. On the inside the alter section is also shingled, and the trusses are exposed, as are the rafters and roof boards. There is stickwork vergeboard in each gable end as well as some Gothic style carving, but the rustic character of the church with its exposed framework predominates. Indeed, one of the striking features of the church is the stained glass window in either end wall, both of which feature coastal landscape motifs and are set off magnificently by the minimally ornamented interior.[3]

While "rustic" may be an appropriately descriptive term for work such as this, Emerson's designs were always considerably more polished than what that word might suggest. For example, the original St. Mary's-By-The-Sea in Northeast Harbor exhibited a radically different concept of rustication. Designed by New York architect George Moffette in 1881, that church strove for a more deliberately crude effect in which the vertical siding consisted of plain-cut timber with the bark retained. Unfinished wood was used throughout for ornamentation. Moffette's design was suggestive of the Adirondack architecture of New York which did not find much favor on the Maine coast.[4] Clearly, there were two entirely different concepts of what constituted appropriate architecture in a natural setting, and Emerson never sought an overly contrived rustic effect, which equally suited the wealthy "rusticators."

St. Jude's Episcopal Church, exterior (Richard Cheek).

1. *Mt. Desert Herald*, September 29, 1889.
2. *Mt. Desert Herald*, July 27, 1889. The citation that Emerson was the architect is in the *Mt. Desert Herald*, November 15, 1886. Gunner Hanson, *Not a Common House*, Northeast Harbor, 1981.
3. The window behind the alter is by Tiffany Studios.
4. *American Architect and Building News*, October 8, 1881.

Stickney Cottage, land side, circa 1920 (Courtesy of Mrs. Marshall Green).

Albert Stickney Cottage

GERRISH ISLAND
KITTERY
1887-88
DESTROYED IN 1975

Albert Stickney, a Harvard educated New York lawyer and author of several books on politics and current affairs, was one of the first to build a summer cottage on Gerrish Island opposite Portsmouth Harbor. If he was hoping to initiate a large development, he was disappointed, as no substantial summer colony ever took hold in Kittery. The open and flat terrain of this site seemed to call for a low-slung cottage firmly planted on a wind-swept undulating landscape. Emerson's design for this project in many ways epitomized the Shingle Style.[1] Historical motifs are almost non-existent in a carefully crafted shingled exterior where the play of light on solids and voids must have seemed to transform this house over the course of a day. Although barely evident in the photographs, even the gable end is angled in a fashion so that its facets appear almost illusionary. In no other project did Emerson succeed so well in exploiting the plastic character of Shingle Style design.

A set of two exterior photographs and four interior views provide the only record of this remarkable design. The integration of the service wing was particularly effective and included an unusual solution to the aesthetic problem of decks. At the end of the wing was a shingled wall with a gate that led onto a deck with railings and lattice on the ocean side. The elevation facing the water, which was not intended to be seen in the same way as the land facade, was not as neatly composed and presented a more irregular appearance.

Stickney Cottage, ocean side, circa 1920 (Courtesy of Mrs. Marshall Green).

Stickney Cottage, circa 1920,
dining room leading toward parlor (top),
hall looking toward dining room (bottom)
(Courtesy of Mrs. Marshall Green).

The interior was sparsely decorated. Plaster was apparently used for the bedroom walls, but the ground floor had horizontal tongue-and-groove paneling decorated in selective areas with vertical studs. In the dining room these studs formed a grid backdrop for the stylized Colonial Revival mantel and over-mantel. Period photographs reveal an open flow of space between the principal first floor rooms, with the parlor at a slightly higher level than the dining room and hall.

"Aunt Molly", the *Portsmouth Chronicle's* Kittery correspondent, observed the progress of construction which began after an old house on the site was demolished in February, 1888.[2] Upon completion of the cottage in June, she noted that, "If Mr. Stickney's object was to have something odd for a summer residence, he has it without doubt. It is the most perfectly unique place on the coast."[3]

1. The source that Emerson designed this cottage was architect John Mead Howells, a summer resident of Kittery who conveyed the information to the owner, Mrs. Edward Crocker. Letter from Mrs. Edward Crocker to Earle G. Shettleworth, Jr., August 9, 1979, Maine Historic Preservation Commission, Augusta. After standing vacant and neglected for fourteen years, the cottage was demolished for a modern replacement.

2. *Portsmouth Daily Chronicle*, February 9, 1888; March 17, 1888; March 29, 1888.

3. *Ibid.*, June 19, 1888. Despite apparent misgivings, "Aunt Molly" approved of the house: "One room, octagon shaped, with the quaintest windows facing south, took our fancy. It is the gem of the rooms. The mantels are the most delightful ones imaginable, with odd little shelves for curiosities."

Stickney Cottage, parlor, circa 1920 (Courtesy of Mrs. Marshall Green).

Unitarian Church

LEDGELAWN AVENUE

BAR HARBOR

1888-89

DESTROYED IN 1978

Emerson designed three churches in Bar Harbor: St. Sylvia's Catholic Church, the Congregational Church, and the Unitarian. All three showed a versatility of styling in the architect's ecclesiastical work. The use of shingles and Colonial Revival motifs placed the Unitarian Church closer to St. Sylvia's than to the Congregational. For this building the nave was parallel to the road with a long stone porch across the facade forming a porte cochere. There were three carriage platforms at each door, evidencing that the parishioners of this church did not arrive on foot. Their upper class status is confirmed by the list of worthies who spoke at its dedication. They included the Reverend Edward Everett Hale, the Reverend Francis G. Peabody, and the Reverend Samuel A. Eliot.[1]

Unitarian Church, *Bar Harbor Record* (Courtesy of the Bar Harbor Historical Society).

Emerson prepared the plans in November, 1888, and construction began in December.[2] The church was dedicated in June, 1889. The tower, with its dome and neo-classical belfry, was visually balanced by a large gabled dormer with concentric rows of saw-tooth shingles above the sash. This dormer only indirectly lighted the interior through a screen in the nave roof. In order to preserve the lines of the paneled ceiling, the dormer was closed off with access through a scuttle above the porte cochere. This was a clear instance of interior utility sacrificed for an exterior design feature.

Newspaper comment at the time was somewhat ambivalent regarding Emerson's Unitarian Church. The *Record* commented, "The whole exterior is shingled but has received no paint. It is fast taking on the old weather-stained appearance that is the idea of the architect".[3] In an earlier comment the same paper stated, "the building is odd looking, but quite pretty, though we do not admire the bare shingles".[4]

The church was entered through three pairs of double doors hung with strap hinges. These opened directly into the auditorium, where rows of pews faced the opposite wall. The decoration of the walls consisted of wainscot with diagonal sheathing and plaster colored with a distemper paint. An enlarged apse on the west side contained the choir and organ loft, the pulpit platform, and the pastor's room. With this orientation toward the long back wall that was parallel to the street, the plan suggested inspiration from vernacular early eighteenth century New England meetinghouses.

There were not enough Unitarians in Bar Harbor to use the church year round when it was built. The congregation dwindled over the years until it was finally dissolved in 1959. After a few years as a Pentecostal church, the vacant building was demolished for town houses.

1. *Mt. Desert Herald*, June 7, 1889.
2. *Bar Harbor Record*, November 15, 1888; December 6, 1888.
3. *Bar Harbor Record*, May 1, 1890.
4. *Bar Harbor Record*, March 7, 1889.

Unitarian Church, 1977 (Maine Historic Preservation Commission).

Congregational Church, circa 1890 (Maine Historic Preservation Commission).

Congregational Church

MT. DESERT STREET

BAR HARBOR

1888-89

BURNED IN 1942

The contrast between the Congregational Church and the Unitarian and Catholic ones could not have been greater. It can only be presumed that the Congregationalists wanted a substantial masonry edifice similar to what was being erected in large cities all across the country. Emerson obliged with a Romanesque design quite unlike the rest of his Maine projects. The congregation had first built a traditional wooden meetinghouse during the mid-nineteenth century. In August, 1888, they apparently consulted Boston architects Andrews & Jacques (who had just opened an office in Bar Harbor) about enlarging the old structure.[1] By October that idea was given up, and Emerson was hired to prepare plans.[2] The nearly completed building was described in the *Record* on May 9, 1889.[3]

The locally obtained red granite was quarry-faced, which gave the exterior a rough texture. The main section of the church, a nave with a crossing, was as close as any Emerson project came to emulating the great architect of the Romanesque Revival style, H. H. Richardson. The clearly articulated fenestration in combination with the quarry-faced stone was similar to that distinguished designer's work. This cannot be said of the massive stone porch and adjoining tower, which were not successfully integrated with the main body of the church and seemed excessively contrived for picturesque effect.

According to newspaper descriptions, the interior detailing was also Romanesque and included clustered columns supporting exposed roof trusses of oak. The predominant colors were olive green and turquoise.[4]

In 1910 a vestry room was added to the rear. The architect is not known.[5] When the Congregational Church was destroyed by fire in 1942, it was replaced by a traditional wooden Colonial Revival style building.

1. *Bar Harbor Record*, August 10, 1888.
2. *Bar Harbor Record*, October 4, 1888.
3. *Bar Harbor Record*, May 9, 1889; April 17, 1890.
4. *Bar Harbor Record*, May 23, 1889.
5. *Bar Harbor Record*, March 23, 1910.

Blake Cottage and Carriage Barn, circa 1895 (Maine Historic Preservation Commission).

Blake Cottage (Richard Cheek).

Thomas D. Blake Cottage

Thomas Blake owned the Blake Steam Pulp Works in Cambridge, a firm whose president, William Stover, hired Emerson to design the large inn at Blue Hill. Blake's summer cottage is located in a community with a long history of settlement and a small but well established summer colony. Construction of the cottage by Eben Mayo of Blue Hill began in October, 1891.[1] The house was probably finished by early in the next year. Blueprints of elevations and floor plans are in the possession of the present owners.[2]

By 1891 the use of the gambrel roof had become an established feature of Emerson's architectural vocabulary. In part this was a response to the growing popularity of the Colonial Revival style. While Emerson himself did much to promulgate the merits of this country's architectural heritage, he consistently avoided the conventional solutions of square, hipped roof structures with columned porches and symmetrical plans. Although the Blake Cottage is one of his more conservative designs and includes such standard treatments as Palladian windows in each gable end and Tuscan porch columns, the house remains essentially a free interpretation of Colonial motifs.

The conservatism of the house for Thomas Blake is in some respects more apparent than real. The first floor plan suggests traditional early nineteenth century room arrangements with its central hallway flanked by a living room and den and leading to the dining room and kitchen in the rear of the house. In fact, although the hallway is narrow, not a "living hall", it forms the crossing between the entrance and dining room on one axis, and the staircase and living room on the other. As a result there is an openness which, in a

PERKINS STREET

CASTINE

1891-92

First floor plan of the Blake Cottage by William R. Emerson (Courtesy of Edward and Ann Miller).

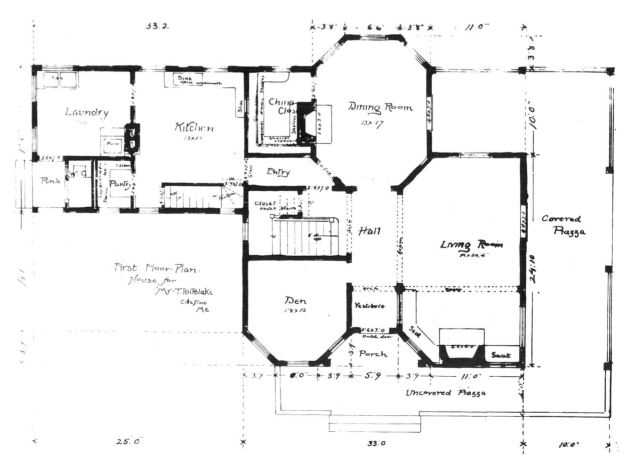

Blake Cottage, living room (Richard Cheek).

small-scale house, encourages the easy access between rooms that had become a hallmark of summer homes. The location of the staircase, however, reflects the architect's increasing tendency to de-emphasize its importance in spatial arrangements.[3]

The principal elevation faces the driveway with a broad gambrel roof extending down to incorporate both the small recessed entrance porch and the long side veranda facing the ocean. The flared shingles above the entrance combine with the two columns to create the illusion of a porch on the land side, where in fact there is an open veranda with a shingled railing. The gambrel motif is repeated in the half-formed gambrel roof over the service wing, which has its own small porch and single Tuscan column. This wing, along with the second and third story dormers, seem to grow out of the main section of the house.

A large carriage barn is also part of the property. While drawings for this structure do not survive, it is reasonable to suppose that it is Emerson's work.

Two exterior changes have been made to the house. About 1928 the porch was partially enclosed with glass on the end nearest the ocean. More seriously detracting from the integrity of the design is a circa 1945 bathroom extension made to the second floor over the porch facing the ocean. This gabled projection spoils the lines of the gambrel roof. As bathrooms are not lacking in the house, this feature may eventually be removed. Alterations were also made to the carriage barn when an apartment was added about 1951.

1. *Industrial Journal*, Bangor, October 16, 1891.
2. The Maine Historic Preservation Commission has a drawing of a china closet for the Blake Cottage.
3. Cynthia Zaitzevsky noted this in regard to Emerson's Milton residence of 1886. Zaitzevsky, *op. cit.*, p. 26.

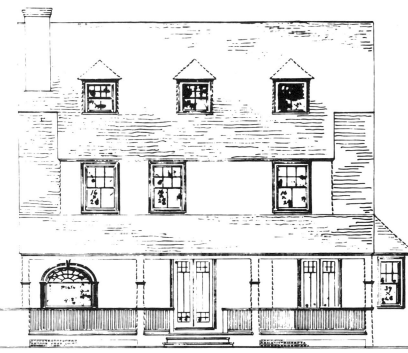

·End· Elevation·

End elevation of the Blake Cottage by William R. Emerson (Courtesy of Edward and Ann Miller).

Blue Hill Inn, circa 1895 (Maine Historic Preservation Commission).

Blue Hill Inn

The Town of Blue Hill contains one of Maine's smaller summer colonies for the wealthy. In 1891, when William Stover commissioned Emerson to design a hotel there, only a few large cottages had been built. Stover, as president of the Blake Steam Pulp Works in Cambridge, Massachusetts, would have been aware of the architect's design at the same time for a cottage in Castine for Thomas Blake, owner of the company. Work began in November, 1891, under the direction of local builder Eben W. Mayo. The Inn was completed in the spring of 1892.[1] The Blue Hill Historical Society owns a collection of working drawings. Although by no means complete, this collection is the most extensive for an Emerson project in Maine.[2]

Blue Hill Inn, circa 1910 (Maine Historic Preservation Commission).

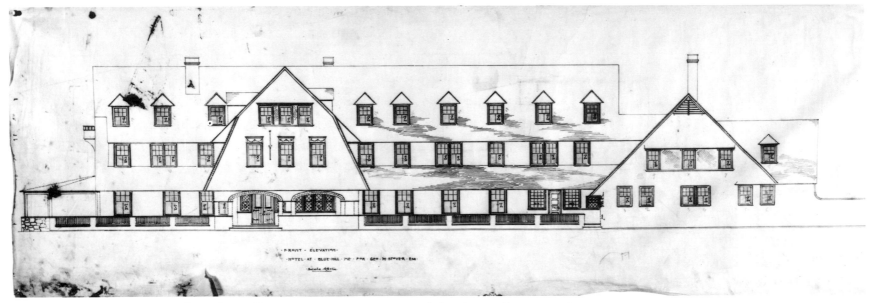

Land elevation of the Blue Hill Inn by William R. Emerson (Courtesy of the Blue Hill Historical Society).

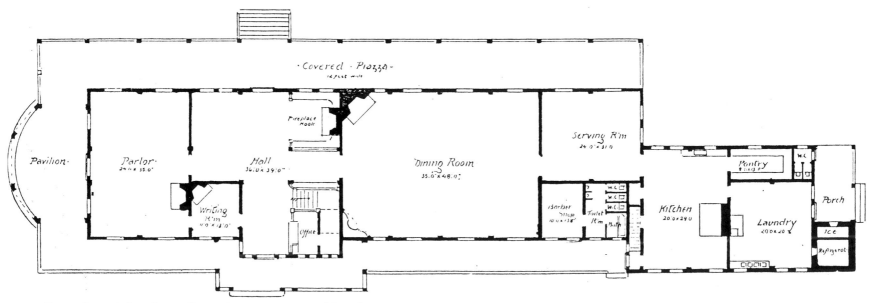

First floor plan of the Blue Hill Inn from promotional brochure (Maine Historic Preservation Commission).

As with the Blake Cottage in Castine, the gambrel roof of the Blue Hill Inn was the single dominating feature of the design. The use of banks of shed roof dormers on the second floor level and rows of gable roof dormers at the third floor enabled the architect to extend the roof down to just above the first story. With so little exposed wall surface except in the gable ends, the effect was something akin to a massive low-slung barn.

As this was a hotel and not a barn, Emerson was careful to relieve the imposing character of the shingled surfaces by sensitive use of Colonial Revival ornament and variations in textures. Subtleties in such details had become especially important where simple square-cut shingles had replaced the variety of patterns employed for many of the Bar Harbor cottages. Evidence of the architect's ability to create textures can be seen in the gable end which extended over the main entrance. Above the second floor windows were festoons, while on the wall surface below the sash billowed out to form a shelter for the segmental arch entrance porch. On the north end the most prominent decorative feature was the Palladian window and shingled balcony at the third story level. On the ground below the porch projected out on a stone base in a polygonal shape, distinguished from the long veranda in the plan as a "pavilion", which opened off the parlor.

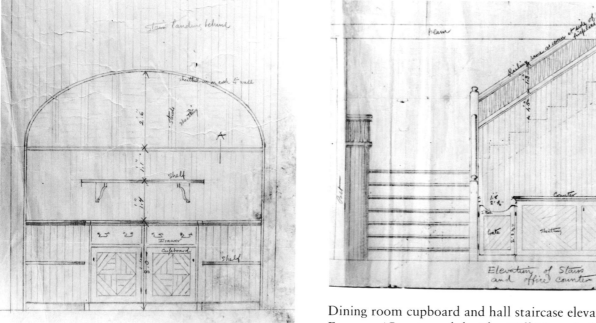

Dining room cupboard and hall staircase elevations by William R. Emerson (Courtesy of the Blue Hill Historical Society).

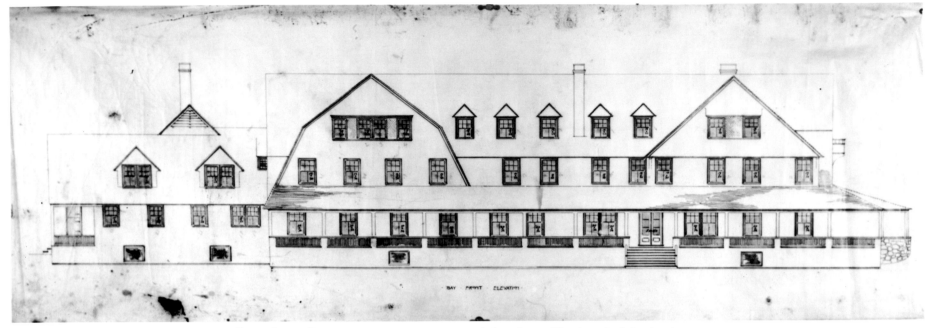

Ocean elevation of the Blue Hill Inn by William R. Emerson (Courtesy of the Blue Hill Historical Society).

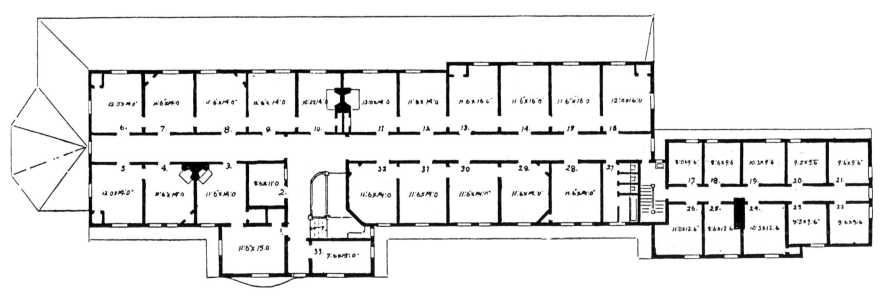

Second floor plan of the Blue Hill Inn from promotional brochure (Maine Historic Preservation Commission).

The interior first floor plan was organized much along the lines of a summer cottage. The entrance opened directly into a hall with a staircase and fireplace inglenook (and, in this case, an office). From this central space access could be gained into the parlor and writing room on one side, and the dining room on the other. The use of wood paneling and restrained Colonial style moldings designed by Emerson was also typical of his cottages by this time. Vertical wood sheathing was relieved by sections of wood panels or brickwork above fireplaces in diagonal or horizontal patterns. Emerson also provided four inch scale drawings for the dining room andirons.

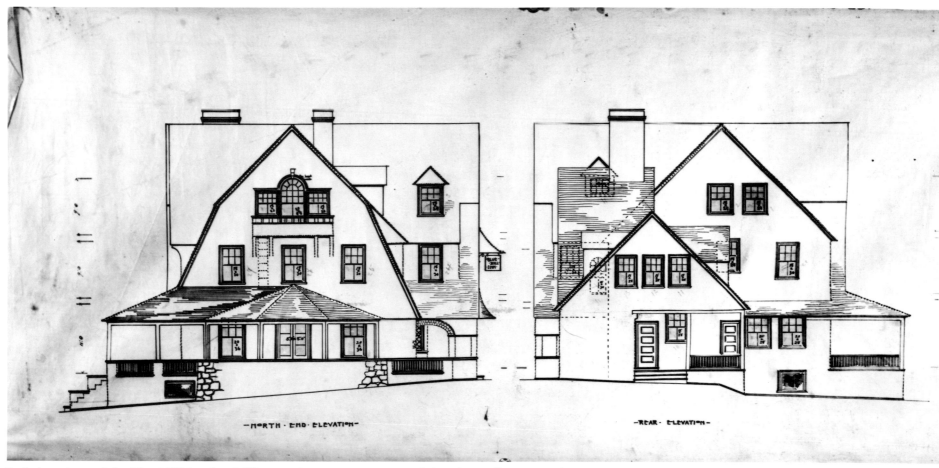

End elevations of the Blue Hill Inn by William R. Emerson (Courtesy of the Blue Hill Historical Society).

Design for fireplace andirons for the Blue Hill Inn by William R. Emerson (Courtesy of the Blue Hill Historical Society).

Included among the drawings are two elevations for a charming shingled "Engine House", which probably contained servants' quarters above. It was characteristic of Emerson to rely on fanciful treatments such as this for small, utilitarian structures.

1. *Industrial Journal*, Bangor, November 20, 1891; *Bar Harbor Record*, January 14, 1892; February 4, 1892. Apparently the laundry room portion of the service wing was not built until 1894. *Ellsworth American*, October 18, 1894.

2. The drawings survived in the house of the contractor, Eben Mayo. Brad Emerson of Blue Hill played an important role in saving these drawings as well as those for Eben Mayo's house.

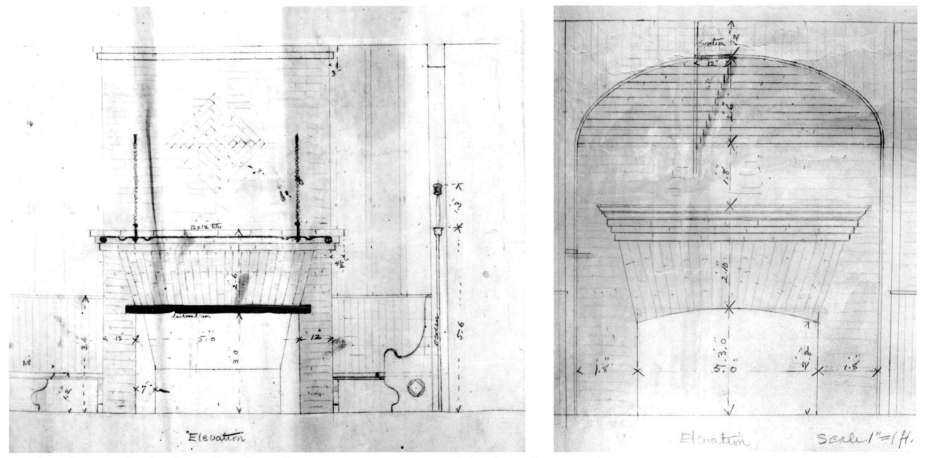

Fireplace elevations for the Blue Hill Inn by William R. Emerson (Courtesy of the Blue Hill Historical Society).

Front · Elevation ·

House · for ·
E · W · Mayo, Esq.
· Blue · Hill · Maine ·

Scale ¼ in = 1 ft ·

Front elevation of the Mayo House by William R. Emerson (Maine Historic Preservation Commission).

Eben W. Mayo House

BEECH HILL ROAD

BLUE HILL

1892

Eben W. Mayo was a leading building contractor in Blue Hill during the nineteenth century. He became acquainted with Emerson as the contractor for the William Blake Cottage and the Blue Hill Inn. Three ink and watercolor elevation drawings document that Emerson was commissioned to design a house for Mayo following the completion of the cottage and the inn. Construction of the house was underway in September, 1892.[1]

Emerson's role in the design of this house may not have extended beyond the set of elevation drawings. The floor plan and interior woodwork are typical of what Mayo himself could have produced in his contracting business. Moreover, the exterior was not built exactly as proposed. Two major departures from the elevations are the absence of a balancing gable end on the ell (which also has a gable roof rather than a hip) and the placement of a chimney toward the middle of the main gable end instead of at the front. Since the chimney placement affects interior arrangements,

Mayo House
(Richard Cheek).

this suggests that Emerson gave some thought to the floor plan, even if his ideas were rejected.[2] Other changes from the house as it stands today may have occurred with later remodelings. These include constructing a base for the oriel window and the absence of eave brackets. The porch posts and railings are recent replacements.

The Mayo House is a curious design, quite unlike the summer cottages with which Emerson is associated. It appears to be an unusual application of British Arts and Crafts influences on a traditional nineteenth century farmhouse plan. As such, it provides an interesting comment on the values of a Maine contractor as opposed to those of the upper class summer residents. The former, in this case, wanted an architect-designed house that was compatible in style and sophistication to suburban residences. The later, when selecting Emerson at any rate, desired a cottage compatible in styling to the vernacular architecture of the region.

1. *Bar Harbor Record*, September 8, 1892: "E. W. Mayo is putting up a two story house and ell for himself." According to Brad Emerson, an older residence on the site was removed a few years later.

2. One interior feature that does suggest the architect's contribution is the placement of the lunette in the dormer on the side of the roof where it is oriented to provide light for the attic stairs.

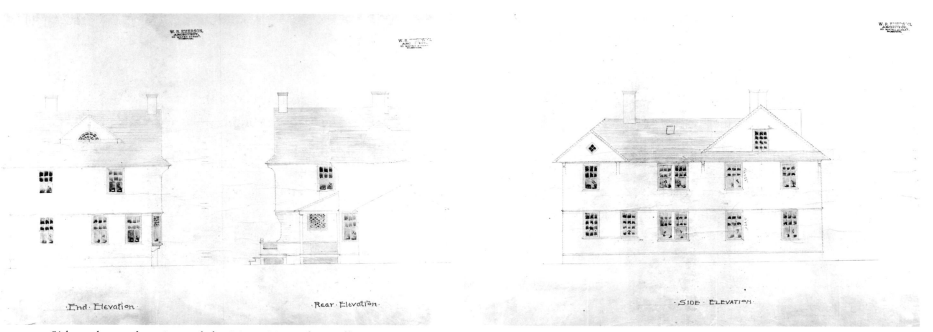

·End·Elevation·   ·Rear·Elevation·   ·SIDE·ELEVATION·

Side and rear elevations of the Mayo House by William R. Emerson (Maine Historic Preservation Commission).

The Crags, Thomas Baily Aldrich Cottage

HARTS NECK

TENANTS HARBOR

1893-94

Thomas Baily Aldrich, a well-known New England writer and the editor of *The Atlantic Monthly*, was characteristic of the clients who sought out Emerson after his popularity declined among fashionable society. Aldrich personally knew of Emerson's work when the architect remodeled his carriage house in Boston for a residence about 1884.[1] His choice of Emerson, and the resulting cottage of unpretentious simplicity, are compatible with the author's romantic sentiments as expressed in a letter to a friend:

I give you twenty guesses at what I am up to. You'll never guess it. I have found my ideal strip of seacoast and am building a bit of a cottage— a cottage in Spain, so to speak, since Spain lies just in front of my proposed piazza. On the left stretch the Camden Hills, twenty-five miles away. It is the wildest and loveliest wave-washed place I ever saw. Tenants Harbor (my land lies outside of the entrance) is a diminutive port with a real custom-house, which doesn't prevent it from being merely a little old-fashioned fishing hamlet, primitive and quaint and unlike anything I know of. I am so happy and dirty as a clam, and enjoy every moment of my working hours in watching the progress of my house, which is to be called, "The Crags"...[2]

Aldrich clearly did not want a large cottage suitable for entertaining society. Presumably, he also wanted a house "primitive and quaint". The client's role is, therefore, particularly important in understanding what was built.

The Aldrich letters document that construction occurred during the winter of 1893-94. According to newspapers, an addition was contemplated in September, 1894.[3] This must refer to the two-story extension to the ell containing a large kitchen and bedroom with balcony above. In 1913 Aldrich's son, Talbot, built an artist's studio on the property. At about the same time a servant's wing and extension to the polygonal room on the north side of the house were built. Neither addition was well integrated with the original design, and they were not by Emerson. The servant's wing was demolished ten years ago. The extension to the north side of the house included a fireplace and still stands.

Emerson's technique of creating a false gambrel roof is very much evident with the Aldrich Cottage. The shingled skirting to create the appearance of a gambrel is employed on all four principal gable ends. It is this that gives the house its Colonial Revival "style", for the ornamentation is otherwise quite vernacular. The arrangement of rooms is planned to maximize the view and includes a living room extending across the front of the house. As was typical by this time, most of the moldings are stock millwork. An important exception is the inglenook fireplace in

The Crags (Richard Cheek).

the living room. A characteristic Emerson feature is what is marked on the plans as a "shelf for lamp" between the living room and the staircase. This space, with leaded glass sash on both sides, provides illumination for the staircase, which otherwise has no direct lighting. In short, The Crags is perfectly suited for its purpose.

1. Zaitzevksy, *op. cit.*, p. 21. Popularly known as "The House of Odd Windows", this Pinckney Street residence is widely admired among those who enjoy Beacon Hill architecture.

2. Aldrich to G. E. Woodbury, August 26, 1893. Ferris Greenslet, *The Life of Thomas Bailey Aldrich*, Boston, 1908.

3. *Ibid.*, see also letter from Aldrich to Woodbury, May 15, 1894. *Industrial Journal*, September 14, 1894. The documentation that Emerson designed this cottage is in the *Rockland Courier-Gazette*, November 10, 1896, and the *Portland Board of Trade Journal*, November, 1893, p. 21. The latter included the following: "It will be a cottage of the old colonial design, plans for which were made by Emerson, the Boston architect. It is said that Mr. Aldrich was recently obliged to decline an invitation to Consul Underwood's farewell reception in Boston 'because of an appointment of long standing with some large sized haddock off the coast of Tenant's Harbor, Maine'."

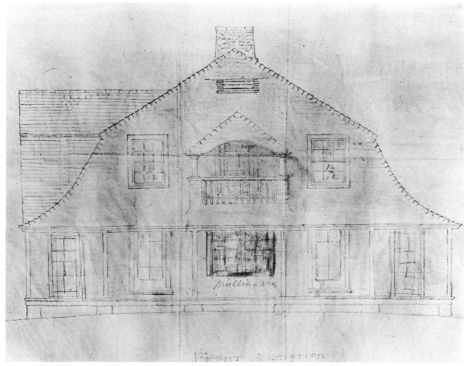

Ocean elevation of The Crags by William R. Emerson
(Courtesy of Janet and Richard Sawyer).

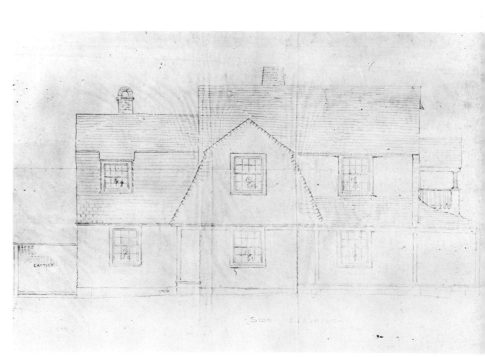

South elevation of The Crags by William R. Emerson
(Courtesy of Janet and Richard Sawyer).

Richardson Cottage, fireplace inglenook, living room (Richard Cheek).

William S. Richardson Cottage

William S. Richardson, a brother-in-law of Thomas Bailey Aldrich, built his cottage next to The Crags. William H. Glover and Company of Rockland began construction in August, 1894, and the house was probably completed before the end of the year.[1] As with the Aldrich Cottage, "primitive and quaint" may have been the operative words. There was a distinct similarity between the Richardson and Aldrich cottages. The original design of the former was documented by Talbot Aldrich in a sketch. From the illustration it is evident there was shingled skirting to create a false gambrel as with the Aldrich cottage. This skirting has been removed from Richardson's house. In doing so, a major character-defining feature of the design has been lost. The playful curve of the serpentine cornice on the south side is reflected in interior details such as the fireplace inglenook and second floor stairhall. Unlike the Crags, this cottage is ornamented with more formal Colonial Revival style woodwork in the main section of the house. Similarly, the first story is clapboarded instead of shingled, and there is a hip roofed wood house connected to the kitchen by a lattice walkway. From 1901 until his death in 1923, Richardson lived in the Beacon Hill carriage house, now popularly known as the "House of Odd Windows", which Emerson remodeled for Aldrich in 1884. He was the inventor of the ball and socket fastener, better known today as a "snap fastener."

1. *Industrial Journal*, Bangor, August 10, 1894; August 24, 1894; September 14, 1894. The citation that identifies Emerson as the architect is in the *Rockland Courier-Gazette*, November 10, 1896.

Sketch of the Richardson Cottage by Talbot Aldrich, July 22, 1898 (Courtesy of Viola and Frederick Sheehan).

Felsted (Richard Cheek)

Felsted, Frederick Law Olmsted Family Cottage

Felsted is a masterpiece of Shingle Style design. It is a culmination of Emerson's work in the sense that it perfectly expresses the evolution of his design concepts for summer cottages. The exterior is eminently suited to its site with an interior equally well arranged. Historical ornamentation is absent, because it would have been superfluous to a composition so exquisitely composed. Thanks to the Frederick Law Olmsted Papers, this is one of Emerson's best documented projects.[1]

By 1896 Frederick Law Olmsted, the noted landscape architect, was in declining health. Concerned about his condition, his wife conceived the idea of building a summer cottage on Deer Isle where the great man could derive therapeutic value by tinkering with the landscape. The family had summered there since 1884, renting farmhouses, so the conditions and absence of society were well known to them.

SEA ELEVATION

Ocean elevation of Felsted by William R. Emerson (Courtesy of the National Park Service, Frederick Law Olmsted National Historic Site).

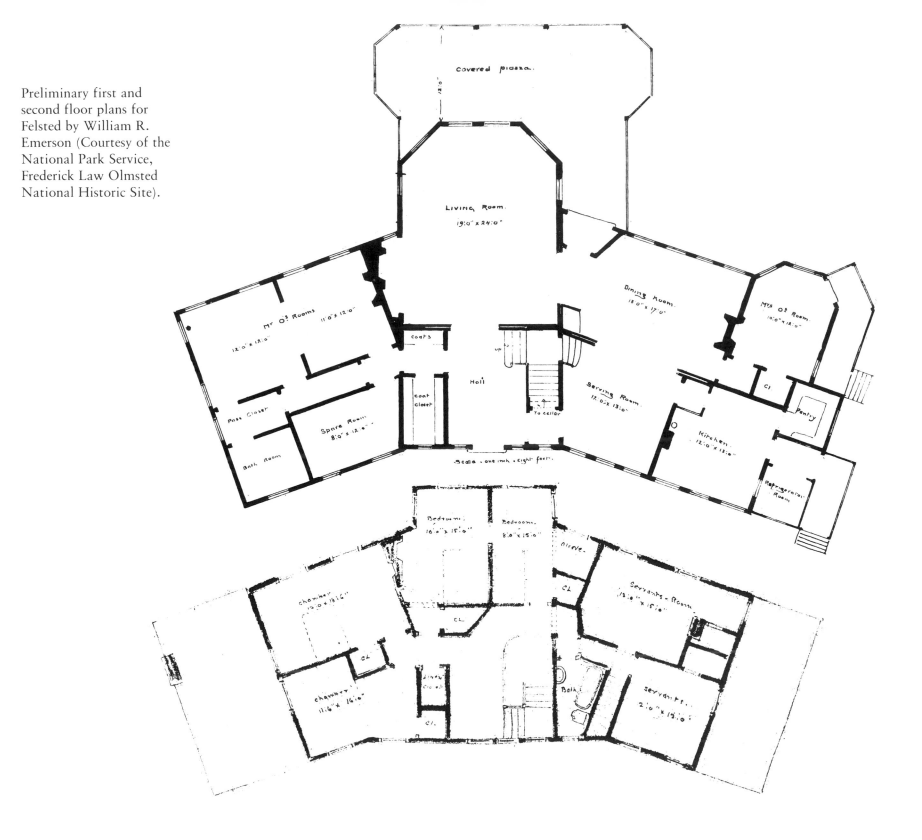

Preliminary first and second floor plans for Felsted by William R. Emerson (Courtesy of the National Park Service, Frederick Law Olmsted National Historic Site).

Frederick Law Olmsted, Jr., took the lead in directing the building campaign, writing to Emerson in April, 1896, to arrange a site visit. It was his half-brother, John Olmsted, who suggested Emerson, as Frederick was apparently not convinced that the idea to build a summer cottage was a good one.[2] Frederick and the architect visited the site on April 26th, and Emerson was directed to make sketches for sister Marian. Frederick wrote to his mother that "I agree with John that a low and rather straggling house would be better than the somewhat boxy plan Marian suggested in her letter in spite of the additional cost for construction and heating."[3] Emerson's instructions included the following program: a bedroom for the senior Olmsted and for an attendant connected with a private bath, a room for Mrs. Olmsted, a spare room for a doctor or guest, a living room, a dining room, pantry, kitchen, and bathroom, all on the ground floor. The piazza was not to extend under the father's room, and all rooms were to be quite small except for the living room. All the interior finish was to be inexpensive and the rooms warm, although not necessarily plastered. The program for the second floor was evidently more flexible.[4]

The architect's preliminary plans are evident in sunprints of several undated floor plans showing variations in room layouts. In these schemes, which must date from May, 1896, the basic arrangement was established. A rectangle, containing the hall and living room, is thrust out over the water. Angled to one side was the wing with

Land elevation of Felsted by William R. Emerson (Courtesy of the National Park Service, Frederick Law Olmsted National Historic Site).

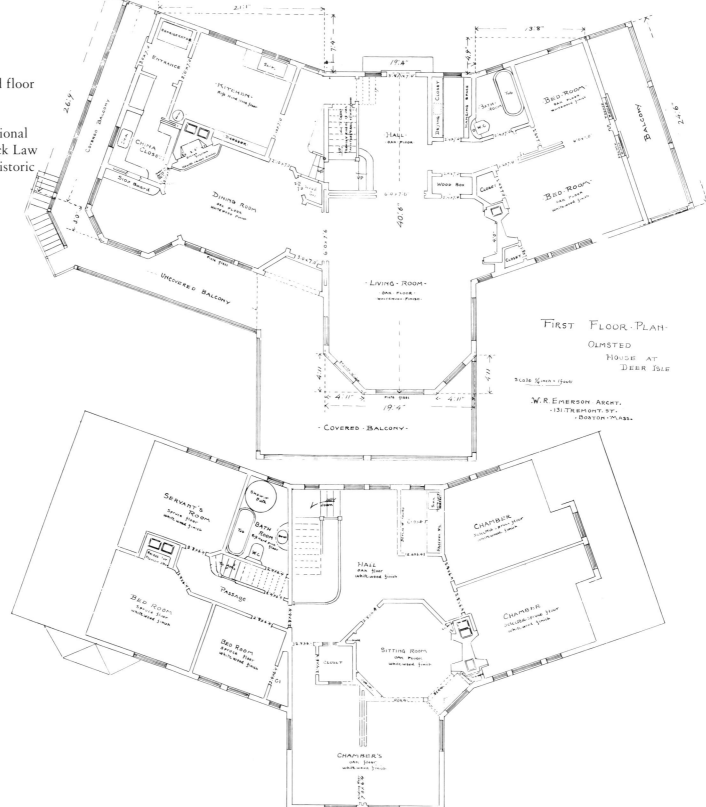

Final first and second floor plans for Felsted by William R. Emerson (Courtesy of the National Park Service, Frederick Law Olmsted National Historic Site).

FIRST FLOOR PLAN

OLMSTED HOUSE AT DEER ISLE

W. R. EMERSON ARCHT.
131 TREMONT ST.
BOSTON MASS.

Olmsted senior's rooms and on the other a wing containing the dining room and kitchen. Mrs. Olmsted's room is shown either adjoining her husband's or at the opposite end of the house in a cramped location between the dining room and kitchen. These schemes were apparently revised following discussions between Frederick, Jr. and his mother in June, 1896. [5] The dining room and kitchen were enlarged at the expense of a "serving room", and Mrs. Olmsted was moved upstairs. Frederick Law Olmsted, Sr.'s wing was opened up and connected to the attendant's room, with a private balcony added.

The changes for the second floor were less significant, with the exception of a new polygonal "sitting room". This room has a curious pyramidal ceiling which was built in order that a lookout on the roof could be added. A lookout was evidently Emerson's suggestion and not very well received by Frederick, who wrote, "I am very much afraid of the appearance of a lookout on the house but if you can make it look right I see no objection." [6] In the end, the idea was rejected.

Emerson suggested that the Rockland firm of William H. Glover and Company be hired to build the house. [7] Construction began in June and was substantially finished by the end of October. [8] Although ready for occupancy in January, 1897, there was a final meeting in April between Frederick, Jr., Emerson, and Glover to discuss the "quality of the finish, etc.". [9] Frederick Law Olmsted, Sr., spent only that first summer at Felsted, as his deteriorating health soon necessitated commitment to a sanitarium. His participation in the design was probably not significant, although much to the surprise of daughter Marian, he requested Emerson to design a garden when the architect and his wife came to dinner. [10] The garden design, which was never built, included a Chinese style serpentine fence.

Felsted displays Emerson's ability to balance distinctly different elements for two opposing elevations. For the ocean front the projecting gable end is fashioned to suggest the stern of a ship. Massive granite blocks support the house so that it stands firmly and prominently at the edge of the rocky shore. Notwithstanding the acute angles of both wings, the land

End elevation of Felsted by William R. Emerson (Courtesy of the National Park Service, Frederick Law Olmsted National Historic Site).

END ELEVATION

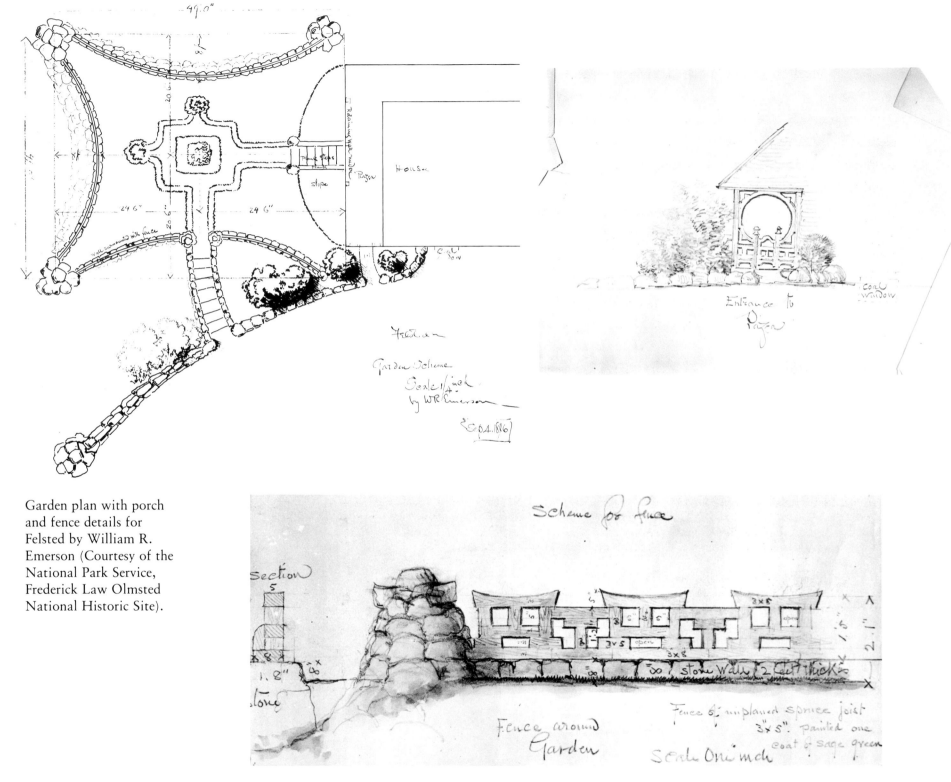

Garden plan with porch
and fence details for
Felsted by William R.
Emerson (Courtesy of the
National Park Service,
Frederick Law Olmsted
National Historic Site).

elevation is barely angled, with the facade encompassed beneath a broad hipped roof. This provides a contrast of quiet repose to the water side which thrusts out over the rocks.

The entry hall, with a staircase typically located at one side, leads directly into the living room and its spectacular view of Penobscot Bay. The woodwork consists of plain vertical pine boards. Such treatment had become characteristic of Emerson's small cottages since the late 1880s as Victorian decor lost favor among his more sophisticated clients.

The Olmsteds made small changes to the house soon after it was completed. The piazza was extended under Olmsted senior's former room, and a sleeping porch was added to the south end. Felsted had a narrow escape from permanent serious alteration when it was converted into a summer hotel in 1926. S. B. Knowlton, the new owner, hired Boston architects Price & Walton to design a large three story wing that extended out from the present kitchen. Although the architects followed Emerson's design motifs, the addition completely spoiled the architectural integrity of the house. Thankfully, Mr. and Mrs. C. L. Pashley purchased the property in 1941 and removed the addition two years later, restoring the original lines of the house.[11]

1. Included among the Felsted drawings at the Frederick Law Olmsted National Historic Site are the following drawings by Emerson: Blueprints for final designs showing four exterior elevations and plans for the first floor, second floor, cellar, and roof; sunprints of several preliminary floor plan schemes; and original paper and tissue drawings for the proposed garden design.

2. Frederick Law Olmsted, Jr. to Emerson, April 18, 1896; Frederick Law Olmsted, Jr. to Mother, May 1, 1896, Frederick Law Olmsted Papers, Library of Congress.

3. Frederick Law Olmsted, Jr. to Emerson, April 26, 1896; Frederick Law Olmsted, Jr. to Mother, May 1, 1896, Olmsted Papers.

4. Frederick Law Olmsted, Jr. to Mother, May 1, 1896, Olmsted Papers.

5. Frederick Law Olmsted, Jr. to Mother, June 10, 1896, Olmsted Papers.

6. Frederick Law Olmsted, Jr. to Emerson, August 26, 1896, Olmsted Papers.

7. Frederick Law Olmsted, Jr. to Mother, May 1, 1896, Olmsted Papers.

8. Ellsworth American, June 4, 1896; September 3, 1896; November 5, 1896.

9. Ellsworth American, January 29, 1897; Frederick Law Olmsted, Jr. to Emerson, April 21, 1897, Olmsted Papers.

10. Diary of Marian Olmsted, entry for August 27, 1896, Olmsted Papers.

11. Mrs. Pashley retains the blueprints for the addition by Price & Walton. The Olmsted National Historic Sites has drawings for modifications to the site, including the addition of a boat house and ice house by the Olmsted firm dating from 1915. These changes were evidently part of an effort by the family to improve the property for sale.

Curtis Cottage, 1897 painting by William R. Emerson (Courtesy of Thuya Gardens, Northeast Harbor).

Joseph H. Curtis Cottage

Joseph Curtis played an important role in the establishment of a summer colony at Northeast Harbor. In a career as a civil engineer, developer, and landscape gardener, Curtis' activities had an impact on other areas of Mt. Desert Island as well. With the construction of a summer cottage in 1882, he led the Boston contingent at Northeast Harbor along with Harvard president Charles Eliot. The first Curtis cottage was a log structure designed by New York architect George Moffette.[1] The overtly rustic style of that structure did not inspire other cottage builders, but it did establish Curtis' own concepts of compatible design for Mt. Desert Island. It was, therefore, consistent with that approach to build a second cottage on his lot patterned after vernacular rural Maine architecture.

Curtis built his second cottage next to the first one in 1897.[2] A painting by William R. Emerson, dated 1897, suggests that the house was his design. The painting is typical of the architect's artistic work at that time. The use of soft, blurred pastels seemed to have been Emerson's preferred medium.[3] The cottage was evidently constructed as it appears in the painting, except for the absence of an east porch, the lack of shingling in the pediments of the roof dormers, and the configuration of the east wall dormer. Alterations in this century by the architectural firm of Shepard and Stearns changed some windows and eliminated such characteristic Emerson touches as the row of saw-tooth shingles at the second floor level. More extensive additions were made to the north side, which is not visible in the painting.

As with so much of Emerson's work, changes to subtle details have a major impact on the integrity of the design. This is especially true with the Curtis Cottage, where the inspiration appears to be more nineteenth century vernacular than seventeenth century Colonial. It it interesting to postulate that Joseph Curtis would have had difficulty in securing another architect to produce a design of this character in 1897, for its inspiration moves beyond the Colonial Revival.

1. *Mt. Desert Herald*, November 16, 1882; *American Architect and Building News*, February 26, 1881.

2. *Ellsworth American*, February 25, 1897. This source states that plans were ready for the contractor by that date.

3. See, for example, "Design for House at Beverly", *Catalogue of the Special Exhibition of the Boston Architectural Club*, 1897, p. 87; "Sketch of An Old Dutch Town" and "Residence at Cincinnati", *Catalogue of the First Annual Exhibition of the Detroit Architectural Club*, April 28-May 12, 1900, pp. 100-101; "Old Monastery, South of France", *Cleveland Architectural Club Catalogue of its Third Exhibition*, May 21-26, 1900, p. 64; "A Memory of Spain", "A Church Interior", and "Sketch", *Catalogue of the Architectural Exhibition Boston Architectural Club*, May 5-19, 1902, pp. 75, 79, 95.

Walker Cottages, Stage Neck (left), Short Sands (center), Grant (right), circa 1900 (Courtesy of the Old York Historical Society).

Three Cottages for Wilson L. Walker

An item in the *New England Master Builder* on March 13, 1897, noted that in York Harbor, "William R. Emerson, 131 Tremont Street, Boston, has plans for three summer cottages to be built this spring for W. L. Walker, grain dealer, here".[1] Walker had at least four rental cottages in this locality, all of which could have been designed by Emerson.

The largest of these, "Cove Cottage", and the smallest, which appears at the right in a turn-of-the-century photograph identified as the "Walker Cottages", are no longer standing. The small one did not even survive long into this century. The photograph of Cove Cottage, whose construction probably pre-dates the others, is not sufficiently clear to identify any distinctly Emerson features except perhaps the circular staircase tower at the intersection of the main block of the house and its wing. Neither cottage can be documented as by W. R. Emerson.

The other two cottages, "Stage Neck" and Short Sands", are still extant but are heavily altered. These are clearly Emerson's work and are part of his 1897 commission. Photographs of the two made by the John Calvin Stevens firm provide the clearest illustrations.[2]

Both cottages are shingled and display minimal ornamentation. The hand of a talented architect is clearly established in considering that both were designed as single family rentals with virtually identical floor plans (excepting the additional ground floor for Stage Neck Cottage), yet their exteriors are very different.[3] Emerson's attention to detail is

Stage Neck Cottage, circa 1920 (Courtesy of John Calvin Stevens II).

Detail of the Short Sands Cottage, circa 1920 (Courtesy of John Calvin Stevens II).

present in the carefully arranged fenestration and the visual relation between the service wing and the main block of the house. In both cases these wings are semi-detached in a manner more suggestive of formal eighteenth century houses rather than the rambling vernacular structures that had long inspired the architect. The result is somewhat novel for nineteenth century summer cottage architecture.

The single family domestic scale of these cottages was a casualty of rising property values and lower standards. The alterations that took place by the 1930s were a result of the desire for more rental units in both structures. Short Sands Cottage is still recognizable, but the introduction of modern windows and an expansion of the third floor has virtually obliterated the original features of Stage Neck Cottage.

1. *New England Master Builder*, Boston, March 13, 1897, p. 14.
2. The Stevens firm was commissioned to design alterations to these cottages in the period of 1910 to 1920. The photographs are in the collection of John Calvin Stevens II.

3. The floor plans, with photographs, of Stage Neck, Short Sands and Cove Cottages are in an extraordinary promotional brochure titled, *York Harbor, Maine*. This undated publication of about 1930 is in the archives of the Old York Historical Society.

Stage Neck Cottage, circa 1920 (Courtesy of John Calvin Stevens II).

Short Sands Cottage, circa 1920 (Courtesy of John Calvin Stevens II).

Clark House (Richard Cheek)

Charles P. Clark House—Additions

PLEASANT STREET

KENNEBUNKPORT

1898

As a child Emerson would have been familiar with the Nathaniel Lord House in the center of Kennebunkport. Erected by housewright Thomas Eaton between 1812 and 1815, this was the home of one of the town's wealthy shipbuilders.[1] In the late nineteenth century Lord's grandson, Charles P. Clark, used the house as a summer home. As president of the New York and New Haven Railroad, Clark lived in New Haven, Connecticut, the remainder of the year. In April, 1898, he hired William R. Emerson to completely redesign the rear wing, which had been rebuilt once before in the mid-nineteenth century. Construction of the $5,000 addition evidently took place over the summer of 1898.[2] Blueprints of the architect's floor plans and elevations survive for this project.

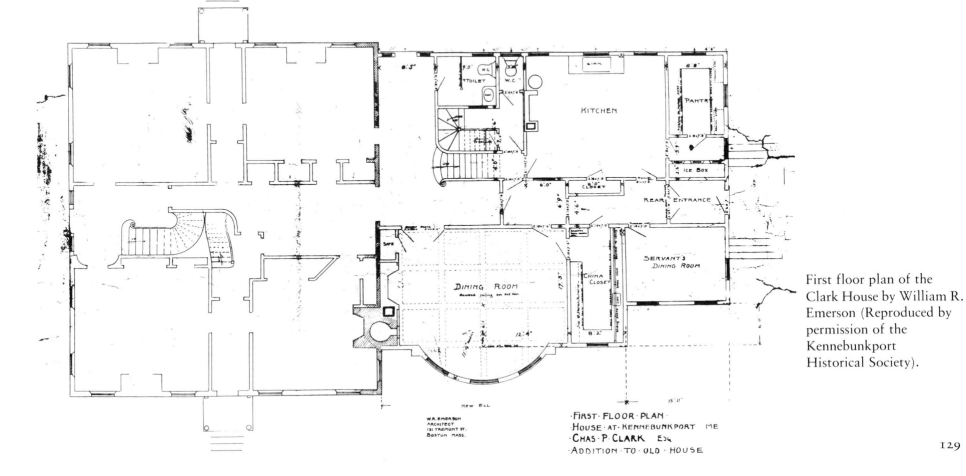

First floor plan of the Clark House by William R. Emerson (Reproduced by permission of the Kennebunkport Historical Society).

For the exterior of the three story addition, Emerson faithfully respected the original detailing of the Federal style house by replicating the original clapboard exposures, cornice moldings, and six-over-six sash. On the west side a new Federal style doorway was also created. At the same time the new wing was subordinated from the main block with a set-back on both side elevations. Moreover, the spacing of the windows, as well as the bowed dining room bay, distinguish the new from the old.

Clark's new wing included a side entry hall and staircase, a dining room, kitchen and service rooms, and a master bedroom on the second floor. Although designed in a neo-Federal style, the interior finish did not replicate Thomas Eaton's original joinery. In the dining room, which had been the kitchen in the previous wing, the early fireplace and bake oven were retained. Embellishments for this room included a curved window seat in the bow window, paneled wainscot, and boxed ceiling beams. These Colonial Revival features are typical of the period and provide a marked contrast to the less formal interior elements found in many of Emerson's cottages. The architect's approach in this instance was completely deferential to one of Kennebunkport's major architectural landmarks.

1. Arthur J. Gerrier, "Thomas Eaton", *A Biographical Dictionary of Architects in Maine*, Vol. V, Number 8, 1988.

2. *Eastern Star*, Kennebunk, April 15, 1898; *New England Master Builder*, Boston, May 17, 1898.

·SIDE ELEVATION·

Side elevation of the Clark House by William R. Emerson (Reproduced by permission of the Kennebunkport Historical Society).

Ocean Point Casino

The documentation for Emerson's involvement in this project rests on a notice in the Bangor trade newspaper, *The Industrial Journal*. In late 1904 a group of Ocean Point property owners met in Waterville with preliminary plans for a building to house a dance hall and bowling alley. It was reported that "the casino will be about 60 x 80 feet and one story high, with a hip roof and a wide veranda will extend around the building". The article further stated that "Architect Emerson of Boston is now making plans for the casino".[1]

According to a 1923 promotional brochure, the casino served as the social center for the summer community at Ocean Point, a peninsula that bounded the eastern side of Boothbay Harbor. Emerson's design is known only through poor-quality exterior photos which show a shingled structure with a broad hip roof and a dormer at each end of the ridge to provide light for the hall. The use of simple, square-cut shingles, slightly flared above the foundation, was characteristic of Emerson's late work.

1. *The Industrial Journal* (Bangor), December, 1904, p. 18. Copies of the Boothbay Harbor newspaper for 1905 have not been located to further document Emerson's involvement with this project.

Ocean Point Casino, circa 1923 (Maine Historic Preservation Commission).

Champernowne Farm, with 1887 ell and stone dairy barn on the left (Richard Cheek).

Champernowne Farm, John Thaxter House

The gambrel roof served as one of the most compelling inspirations for the Colonial Revival style, and Emerson's design for the Thaxter House is perhaps the earliest example of its use as an homage to that eighteenth century American roof form.[1] Indeed, this project offered Emerson his first opportunity to employ what was to become his favorite design motif for the Shingle Style.

Levi Thaxter, husband of the poet Celia Thaxter, built this house principally for their son John. The younger Thaxter's ambition was to establish a small farm on the coast near the Isles of Shoals where his parents summered. The house also served as the principal residence for the entire family. A deep interest in the history of the site, particularly its first occupant, Francis Champernowne, motivated the Thaxters to build in the tradition of American Colonial architecture.[2]

Unlike the gambrels Emerson later designed, however, the Thaxter House is almost vertical in its proportions with the lower slope of the roof barely perceptible. This suggests that inspiration was derived from late eighteenth century examples rather than the older one-and-a-half story farm houses built in the earliest settlement period. Indeed, the Cutts House that was on the site, and which is said to have supplied materials for the new structure, may have provided the model.[3] The house also differed from Emerson's later work in that the walls are sheathed in clapboards rather than shingles.

When John Thaxter married in 1887, he had the house substantially enlarged by adding a cross-gambrel on axis with the main entrance, which was on the land side. The great stone arch supporting a gambrel service wing acted as a porte cochere. A stone dairy barn was also built at that time. This work and the house his brother Roland Thaxter built nearby can be attributed to Emerson.[4]

In recent years the front of the Thaxter House has been altered and the stone dairy barn converted into a residence. Roland Thaxter's house had a round arched service wing of its own added in 1892.

1. This project was brought to my attention by Robben McAdam as this book was about to go to press.
2. *Aunt Rozzie Remembers,* by Rosamond Thaxter, circa 1981, privately printed, pp. 5-6.

3. The staircase wainscott, for example, may derive from the Cutts House. Another possible source is the Goodman House in Lenox, Massachusetts, published in the *American Architect and Building News* in October 1877. My thanks to Richard Candee for pointing out this connection.
4 This assumption is supported by the fact that Roland Thaxter hired Emerson to design his Cambridge house in 1891.

The Projects: Part II

The following projects were either not built, are lacking sufficient documentation, or have no illustrations.

United States Post Office Building

PORTLAND   1866   NOT BUILT

As a young man of thirty-three in practice alone for the first time, William R. Emerson evidently made an effort to secure the commission for the new post office building in Portland after the fire of July 4, 1866. A local newspaper referred to Emerson as the "U. S. Architect", suggesting he was working for the Treasury Department: "We understand from Mr. Emerson, that his plans will all be matured in a few weeks, for the new building, which will be an entirely different structure from the present one."[1] In the end a new structure was designed by Treasury architect Alfred B. Mullett.

1. *Portland Daily Press*, August 11, 1866. Research by Denys Peter Myers has failed to locate any documentation that Emerson worked for the Treasury Department.

Edenfield, General and Mrs. William A. Smith Cottage

DUCK BROOK   BAR HARBOR   1881   DESTROYED

Samuel E. Lyons of New York built his first cottage in this vicinity in 1869. In 1881 he commissioned William R. Emerson to design a second cottage for his daughter and son-in-law, General William A. Smith.[1] Lyons erected a third cottage, Brookend, in 1884, which was also designed by Emerson. After the construction of the first two cottages, the newspapers are not clear who used which cottage or if other parties were involved as occupants of Lyons' three residences. This situation is further complicated by the fact that Lyons hired Emerson to design yet another structure in 1886.

The only photographs of "Edenfield" post-date the extensive remodeling undertaken by Mrs. Miles Carpenter in 1898-99. She renamed the cottage "Hautereve". The architects for this work were Andrews, Jacques & Rantoul of Boston.[2]

1. *Bar Harbor Tourist*, June 11, 1881.
2. *Bar Harbor Record*, December 14, 1898.

Fernierest, Mrs. W. F. Cochrane Cottage

SHORE PATH   BAR HARBOR   1882   DESTROYED IN 1903

Mrs. Cochrane of Yonkers, New York, announced plans to erect a cottage in April, 1882.[1] No illustrations have been located of this short-lived structure. Emerson also designed a remodeling of the cottage in 1892 for Charles W. Beigner of Philadelphia.[2] Upon demolition, Fernierest was replaced by another cottage.

1. *Mt. Desert Herald*, April 29, 1881. Emerson is identified as the architect in a list of cottages and their architects, *Bar Harbor Record*, March 17, 1887.
2. *Bar Harbor Record*, September 8, 1892.

Hotel for E. G. Des Isle

ISLE AU HAUT   1882   NOT BUILT?

Isle Au Haut is one of the most reclusive summer colonies in the Penobscot Bay area. During the 1880s a small number of Shingle Style cottages were built on one section of the island. Initially, however, some investors contemplated a larger development. In the spring of 1882 E. G. Des Isle, a Bar Harbor hotel owner, attempted to raise $20,000 to build a hotel on Isle Au Haut. Emerson was hired to design a structure with one hundred rooms.[1] It is unlikely that this hotel was built, for Isle Au Haut never experienced development on that scale.[2] Des Isle did build a "tourist home" in 1886, but that burned in September, 1887.[3]

1. *Mt. Desert Herald*, April 22, 1882.
2. Kevin Murphy, "Ernest W. Bowditch", *A Biographical Dictionary of Architects in Maine*, Vol. V, No. 3, 1988.
3. *Mt. Desert Herald*, September 2, 1887.

Charles H. Parker Cottage (Remodeling)

BLUE HILL   1884   NOT BUILT?

A single newspaper reference in the *Mt. Desert Herald* notes that Emerson was hired to remodel a cottage for Charles H. Parker, president of the Suffolk Savings Bank in Boston.[1] Blue Hill did have a small summer colony, concentrated in part on a peninsula known as "Parker Point". No record of this cottage, however, has come to light.

1. *Mt. Desert Herald*, August 15, 1884.

Samuel E. Lyons Cottage

DUCK BROOK   BAR HARBOR   1886   BURNED IN 1886

Samuel Lyons hired Emerson for a third cottage in 1886. It is not clear if this was intended for rental purposes or was built to be sold.[1] In any case, the almost finished house was sold to Mrs. George P. Bowler in November, 1886.[2] The next month it was destroyed in a fire.[3] Mrs. Bowler commissioned her architects, Rotch & Tilden of Boston, to design a new cottage, Corfield, which was built on the site.[4]

1. *Mt. Desert Herald*, November 19, 1886.
2. *Ibid.*, November 19, 1886.
3. *Ibid.*, December 10, 1886. Lyons died in January, 1887.
4. *Ibid.*, September 23, 1887.

Graystone, Cary Lea Cottage

DUCK BROOK VICINITY   BAR HARBOR   1886-87   DESTROYED IN 1932 OR 1933

The only record of this cottage is a long newspaper description published after its completion in 1887.[1] The description reveals that Graystone was shingled and had elaborate stonework supporting the structure on its hilly site above Eden Street. This account describes a large house with a variety of treatments for the numerous windows and dormers, a porte cochere, and a sizable veranda. Included in the floor plan was a laboratory off the study for Cary Lea, who was a chemist. Lea's winter residence was Chestnut Hill, outside of Philadelphia.

1. *Bar Harbor Record*, March 24, 1887. Emerson is also mentioned as the architect in the *Mt. Desert Herald*, November 5, 1886.

Chatwold, Joseph Pulitzer Cottage (Additions)

BAR HARBOR   1895   NOT BUILT

Designed in 1883 by Rotch & Tilden, Chatwold underwent several enlargements after it was acquired by the New York newspaper publisher Joseph Pulitzer. The Tudor style mansion was first expanded by architects Andrews, Jacques & Rantoul in 1894. In September, 1895, the *Record* revealed that, "Mr. Joseph Pulitzer has engaged Architect W. S. Emerson [sic] of Boston, who is now laying out plans for extensive alterations at Chatwold. The portion of Chatwold recently finished is not satisfactory to the owner and it is to be remodeled."[1]

Evidently Pulitzer was not happy with Emerson's solution, for by October he had hired the New York firm of McKim, Mead & White to prepare plans.[2] Over the next several years this firm completed the remodeling of Chatwold. "Mr. Pulitzer", the paper reported, "means that he will have Chatwold to his liking whatever the cost may be."

1. *Bar Harbor Record*, September 4, 1895.
2. *Bar Harbor Record*, October 9, 1895.

Bar Harbor Hospital

1898   NOT BUILT

In 1897 the Bar Harbor Village Improvement Association appointed a committee of resident and non-resident physicians to prepare a report on the need for a new hospital. With many wealthy summer residents, good medical facilities were considered essential for the prestigious summer colony. According to one source, "the committee's efforts in raising money met with such success that... prominent architects were invited to submit plans for the proposed building."[1] It can be presumed that Emerson was among those interested in the project as another newspaper reported that, "Plans for the new hospital by W. R. Emerson, architect, are in the hands of the builders for estimates." The hospital's building committee included Dr. Robert Amory of Brookline, a long-standing Emerson client who would have been familiar with the architect's new Bournewood Hospital in Brookline, built in 1897.[2] In the end, the hospital committee, which also consisted of James S. Kennedy, William Fennelly, Andrew Rodick, and George Dorr, selected local architect Milton W. Stratton.

1. *Bar Harbor Record*, July 13, 1898; December 28, 1898.
2. *Ellsworth American*, April 20, 1898.

Projects Outside Maine

BY WILLIAM R. EMERSON

This list updates and expands that which was prepared by Cynthia Zaitzevsky in 1969. Much of this information derives from Dr. Zaitzevsky's subsequent research which she generously shared with me. I also wish to thank the following individuals for assisting in identifying these projects: Earle G. Shettleworth, Jr.; Sally Zimmerman, Cambridge Historical Commission; Edith Clifford, Milton Historical Society; Mary Donohue, Connecticut Historical Commission; Teresa D. Cederholm, Boston Public Library; Greer Hardwicke, Brookline Historic Preservation Commission; Duscha Scott, Newton Historical Society; Nicholas Langhart, Clark University; John Pomaranc, Commission on Chicago Landmarks; James Garvin, Division of Historical Resources, New Hampshire; and Steven C. Gordon, Ohio Historical Society. The following sources are abbreviated as follows:

AABN — *American Architect and Building News* (Boston)

BAI — Boston Architectural Index (Fine Arts Department, Boston Public Library)

BHC — Brookline Historical Commission

BSA — Boston Society of Architects

CHC — Cambridge Historical Commission

FLO — Frederick Law Olmsted Papers, Library of Congress

IANR — Inland Architect and News Record (Chicago)

OA — Olmsted Associates Papers, Library of Congress

ONHS — Olmsted National Historic Site, Brookline

CONNECTICUT
William Erastus Collins House, c. 1890
Hartford, Destroyed
Source: *IANR*, Vol. 16, No. 1, August, 1890

"Meadow Court," Mrs. Charles S. Guthrie House, 1901-03
New London, Extant
Source: OA; ONHS; *American Homes and Gardens*,
September, 1912, 308-310

DISTRICT OF COLUMBIA
Elephant House Project, National Zoo, 1890
Washington, D.C., Not Built
Source: FLO Papers, ONHS; Smithsonian Institution

ILLINOIS
George S. Willits House, 1889-90
Pine and Erie Streets, Chicago, Destroyed
Source: *IANR*, Vol. 15, No. 4, May, 1890

MASSACHUSETTS
BARNSTABLE
St. Mary's Episcopal Church, 1890
Main Street, Extant
Source: Church Records

BELMONT
Belmont Library, 1902
Pleasant Street, Extant (now school offices)
Source: Town Records

BEVERLY
Alexander Cochrane House, 1880-81
Prides Crossing, Extant
Source: *AABN*, June 25, 1881

Charles G. Loring House, 1881
Prides Crossing, Extant
Source: *AABN*, October 4, 1884

William Caleb Loring House, 1887
Prides Crossing, Burned in 1970
Source: FLO; ONHS

St. Margaret's Catholic Church, 1887
Hale Street, Beverly Farms, Extant
Source: *Beverly Citizen*, July 16, 1887

"Design for a House at Beverly"
Unlocated
Source: Painting published in Catalogue of BSA, 1897

BOSTON
Four Town Houses, 1859 (Preston & Emerson)
31-37 Hancock Street, Extant
Source: *Architects and Mechanics Journal* (New York),
Vol. I, October, 1859, p. 5

Rice Grammar School, 1868-69 (Emerson & Fehmer)
Dartmouth and Appleton Streets, Extant
Source: BAI

Creighton House, 1869-70 (Emerson & Fehmer)
245-47 Tremont Street, Destroyed
Source: Bainbridge Bunting: *Houses of Boston's Back Bay*
(1969)

Sherwin Grammar School, 1869-70 (Emerson & Fehmer)
Windsor and Sterling Streets, Destroyed
Source: BAI

Two Town Houses, 1871 (Emerson & Fehmer)
122-24 Commonwealth Avenue, Extant
Source: Bunting, *Houses, op. cit.*

Town House, 1871 (Emerson & Fehmer)
126 Commonwealth Avenue, Extant
Source: Bunting, *Houses, op. cit.*

Town House, 1872 (Emerson & Fehmer)
84 Commonwealth Avenue, Extant
Source: Bunting, *Houses, op. cit.*

Town House, 1872 (Emerson & Fehmer)
192 Commonwealth Avenue, Destroyed
Source: Bunting, *Houses, op. cit.*

Two Town Houses, 1872 (Emerson & Fehmer)
114-116 Commonwealth Avenue, Extant
Source: Bunting, *Houses, op. cit.*

Two Town Houses, 1873 (Emerson & Fehmer)
118-20 Commonwealth Avenue, Extant
Source: Bunting, *Houses, op. cit.*

Granite Stores, 1873 (Emerson & Fehmer)
5 Winthrop Square, Extant
Source: *Architectural Sketch Book* (Boston), September, 1873

Massachusetts Homeopathic Hospital, 1874
East Concord Street, Extant (Additions in 1884, 1892)
Source: *Architectural Sketch Book* (Boston), August, 1874;
October, 1876

Stable for James A. Rieddel & Company, 1878
Newbury and Hereford Streets, Destroyed
Source: BAI

J. P. Greenough House, 1880
15 Greenough Street, Jamaica Plain, Extant
Source: *L'Architecture Americaine*, 1886; *AABN* Building
Intelligence, July 12, 1879, January 10, 1880, March 20, 1880.
Dr. Zaitzevsky believes that other houses built by Greenough
in the immediate vicinity of this one may also be by Emerson.

Two Houses for J. P. Greenough, 1880
Jamaica Plain, Not Built
Source: *AABN*, January 31, 1880 (presumably an early scheme
for the above)

Six Houses for Henry B. Williams, c. 1880
62-72 St. James Avenue, Destroyed
Source: BAI

Boston Art Club, 1880-81
270 Dartmouth Street, Extant
Source: *AABN*, June 3, 1882

James A. Houston House, 1881
Maple Street, Dorcester, Destroyed
Source: *AABN*, Building Intelligence, January 1, 1881

Odd Fellows Hall, 1884
River Street, Dorchester, Not Located
Source: *Milton News*, February 2, 1884

Thomas Bailey Aldrich Carriage Barn (Remodeling), c. 1884
24 Pinckney Street, Extant
Source: Aldrich Family—See Zaitzevsky, *Emerson*

E. M. Huntington House, c. 1885
101 Forest Hills Street, Jamaica Plain, Destroyed
Source: *Engineering Record* (NY), March 19, 1888;
L'Architecture Americaine, 1886

Hasket Derby House, 1886
350 Beacon Street, Extant
Source: BAI

Mary and Emily Rigby House, 1886
207 Savin Hill Avenue, Dorchester, Extant
Source: Present Owners (original drawings)

House (Remodeling), 1890
29 Fairfield Street, Extant
Source: *AABN*, November 5, 1892

Spooner Building, 1891
Centre Street, Jamaica Plain, Destroyed
Source: BAI

Robert M. Morse House, 1893
100 Pond Street, Jamaica Plain, Extant
Source: Boston Building Permit, May 10, 1893

J. Franklin Faxon Building, 1894
Lincoln, Corner of Tufts, Extant
Source: BAI

Houses and Store for Frederick Ayer, 1897
Washington Street, Dorchester, Destroyed
Source: *AABN*, Building Intelligence, July 3, 1897

BOURNE
John Parkinson Cottage, c. 1886
Buzzards Bay, Extant (Additions by 1901)
Source: Stevens & Cobb, *Examples of American Domestic Architecture*, 1889;
IANR, June, 1896 (Dexter Stain Advertisement)

BROOKLINE
Dr. Tappan Eustis Francis House, 1879
35 Davis Street, Extant
Source: *AABN*, February 8, 1879; Brookline Tax Records

Houses on Fisher Hill, 1889
Unlocated
Source: *IANR*, Vol. 13, No. 4, p. 53

George Wales House, 1889
22 Carlton Street, Extant
Source: BHC

Ellen Chapman House, 1891
51 Upland Road, Extant
Source: BCH

Miss Denny House, 1891
65 Upland Road, Extant
Source: BHC

Meade-Bowker Double House, 1895
53-55 Brook Street, Extant
Source: BHC

Bournewood Hospital, 1897
300 South Street, Extant with Alterations
Source: *AABN*, *Building Intelligence*, October 30, 1897; BHC

CAMBRIDGE
John Allyn House, 1886
11 Berkeley Street, Extant
Source: CHC

Lucy Dexter House, 1886-87
76 Sparks Street, Extant
Source: CHC

Mrs. H. M. Saville House, 1887
Concord Avenue, Not Built
Source: CHC

William James House, 1889
95 Irving Street, Extant
Source: CHC

Robert Davis House, 1889
110 Irving Street, Extant
Source: CHC

Roland Thaxter House, 1891
7 Scott Street, Extant
Source: CHC

Mrs. R. A. Richards House, 1895
182 Brattle Street, Extant
Source: CHC

F. R. Richards House, 1895
3 Channing Street, Destroyed
Source: CHC

James Gray House, 1901
12 Walker Street, Extant with Alterations
Source: CHC

CANTON
Augustus Hemenway House, 1882-83
67 Green Street, Extant (Service Wing Destroyed)
Source: *Milton News*, May 28, 1883

COHASSET
Francis V. Balch House, 1881
Sandy Cove, Destroyed
Source: *AABN*, Building Intelligence, February 5, 1881, p. 72

Asa Potter House, 1882
646 Jerusalem Road, Extant with Alterations
Source: *IANR*, 1889, p. 53; *Artistic Houses*, Vol. II, Plate II, 1884

"Stoneleigh," G. T. Braman House, c. 1885
478 Jerusalem Road, Extant
Source: *Sanitary Engineer* (NY), April 16, 1887; *The Builder* (NY), May 11, 1889

"An Interior at Cohassett, Massachusetts," by 1892
Unlocated
Source: *Engineering Record* (NY), April 23, 1892

DARTMOUTH
Mrs. Robert Clifford Watson House, 1903
Mishaum Point, South Dartmouth, Extant
Source: Watson Family (see Zaitzevsky, *Emerson*)

GLOUCESTER
"The Hulk", Studio for William M. Hunt, 1877
Magnolia, Destroyed
Source: *AABN*, February 23, 1878

HAVERHILL
Academy Hall, 1868-70 (Emerson & Fehmer)
Bradford College. Altered
Source: College Archives

"Birchbrow Farm," Thomas Saunders House, 1880
Lake Saltonstall, Demolished in 1946
Source: *AABN*, Building Intelligence, March 10, 1880

HINGHAM
Old Ship Meeting House (Renovations), 1869
Renovations removed
Source: Zaitzevsky, *Emerson*

MANCHESTER
Mrs. Mary Hemenway House, 1884
Manchester-By-The-Sea, Extant
Source: *AABN*, September 27, 1884; George W. Sheldon, *Artistic Country Seats* (NY), 1886-87

MARTHA'S VINEYARD
"Shingled Cottages", by 1889
Unidentified
Source: "William R. Emerson", *Illustrated Boston, The Metropolis of New England*, New York, 1889, p. 153

MILTON
Robert S. Watson House (Remodeling), c. 1872
(Emerson & Fehmer)
Adams Street, Destroyed
Source: Watson Family

"Three Pines", Forbes Sisters House, 1876
7 Fairfax Street, Extant
Source: *Architectural Sketch Book*, April, 1876

"Old Farm," Augustus and Mary Hemenway House (Remodeling), 1877
Canton Avenue, Extant with Extensive Additions
Source: *AABN*, December 22, 1877

William E. C. Eustis House, 1877-78
1426 Canton Avenue, Extant
Source: Eustis Family

John Bancroft House (Remodeling), 1878
Adams Street, Destroyed
Source: *AABN*, November 9, 1878

Town Hall Competition, 1878
Not Built
Source: *AABN*, August 31, 1878

T. R. Glover House, 1879
320 Adams Street, Extant with Extensive Alterations
Source: *AABN*, August 2, 1879

J. Huntington Wolcott House (Interior Alterations), 1880
1733 Canton Avenue, Extant with Extensive Alterations
Source: *AABN*, Building Intelligence, March 20, 1880

William J. Ladd House, c. 1881
267 Adams Street, Extant
Source: *Milton News*, July 8, 1882

Robert C. Watson House, 1882
271 Adams Street, Extant
Source: *Milton News*, August 5, 1882

Edward C. Perkins House, c. 1882
273 Adams Street, Extant with Extensive Alterations
Source: *Milton News*, August 5, 1882

James M. Barnard House, c. 1883
297 Adams Street, Extant with Large Wing Added
Source: John Calvin Stevens Sketch Book, Private Collection;
AABN, August 8, 1885

Col. R. H. Stevenson House and Stable, c. 1884
41 Green Street, Stable Extant
Source: *AABN*, November 8, 1884; November 15, 1884

A. E. Touzalin House, 1884-86
Highland Street, Destroyed
Source: *Milton News*, February 21, 1885; *AABN*, March 12,
1887; *Engineering and Building Record*, June 21, 1890

William R. Emerson House, 1886
201 Randolph Avenue, Extant
Source: *The Builder* (NY), September 14, 1889 (Mistakenly
identified as a residence in Worcester, Massachusetts); Watson
Family

Richard Olney House, 1888
Brush Hill Road, Not Built (?)
Source: OA; ONHS

William H. Forbes House, 1891
172 Adams Street, Extant
Source: Forbes Family

Church of Our Savior, 1903
11 Babcock Street, Extant
Source: Church Records

George Watson House, 1910
216 Randolph Avenue, Extant
Source: Miss Sylvia Watson

NAUSHON ISLAND
"Stone House", William H. Foster Cottage, 1887
Extant
Source: Forbes Family

NEW BEDFORD
William J. Rotch House (Addition), c. 1865-70
19 Irving Street, Extant
Source: *HABS*, Massachusetts, Catalogue 41

E. D. Mandell House, 1883
196 Hawthorn Street, Destroyed
Source: ONHS; Diary of Charles Eliot, Loeb Library, Harvard
University

NEWTON
George D. Hatch House, 1880
Waverly Avenue, Destroyed
Source: *AABN*, Building Intelligence, March 20, 1880; January
8, 1881

Judge John Lowell House, c. 1885
517 Hammond Street, Extant
Source: Dexter Stain Advertisement, *The Brochure Series of
Architectural Illustrations*, 1895; Newton Historical Society

R. H. White House, 1886
Chestnut Hill, Destroyed
Source: Milton Historical Society

Block of Six Stores for William Claflin, 1895
Newtonville, possibly 791-821 Washington Street, Extant
Source: *AABN*, Building Intelligence, September 28, 1895

PETERSHAM
Soloman Lincoln House, 1886
North Main Street, Extant, Service Wing Enlarged
Source: *AABN*, January 23, 1886

RANDOLPH
Stable for Henry A. Belcher, 1892
Not Built (?)
Source: OA; ONHS

SPRINGFIELD
George E. Howard House, 1888
165 Mill Street, Destroyed
Source: Henry-Russell Hitchcock, *Springfield Architecture 1800-1900*, 1980, p. 53.

SWAMPSCOTT
"House at Swampscott", by 1891
Unlocated
Source: *Engineering Record* (NY), July 18, 1891

WORCESTER
Frederick Kimball House, 1887
292 Lincoln Street, Extant
Source: *Engineering and Building Record* (NY), March 7, 1888

House for Francis Lincoln, 1893
61 William Street, Extant
Source: *Engineering and Building Record* (NY), September 16, 1893. The Edward Lincoln House (1886) at 36 Sever Street may also be by Emerson.

UNLOCATED (MASSACHUSETTS)
"At Highlands," Unidentified House, c. 1880
Source: John Calvin Stevens Sketch Book, Private Collection

NEW HAMPSHIRE
Charles L. Richardson House, 1891
Maple Street, Manchester, Destroyed
Source: *The Mirror's Pictoral Manchester*, Manchester, 1896

"Mapleknoll," Frank H. Shapleigh House, 1897
Jackson, Extant
Source: Blueprints (Present Owners)

Jackson Public Library, 1900-01
Route 16A, Jackson, Extant (Moved in 1930)
Source: Library Records

NEW YORK
Nelson B. Chapman House, 1887
Gilbertsville, Extant in 1970
Source: Owner's Research in Local Newspaper

Battle Monument, U. S. Military Academy, Competition, 1890
West Point, Not Built
Source: *AABN*, December 13, 1890

OHIO
Unidentified House, by 1900
Cincinnati, Unlocated
Source: Published as "Residence at Cincinnati", *Catalogue of the First Annual Exhibition of the Detroit Architectural Club*, April 28-May 12, 1900

RHODE ISLAND
M. H. Sanford House, 1869-70 (Emerson & Fehmer)
72 Washington Street, Newport, Extant
Source: Downing and Scully, *The Architectural Heritage of Newport, Rhode Island*, Cambridge, 1952, p. 134

Mary Channing Eustis House, 1882-83
336 Gibbs Avenue, Newport, Extant in 1982
Source: Jordy and Monkhouse, *Buildings on Paper, Rhode Island Architectural Drawings 1825-1945*, Providence, 1982, p. 60

"Five Shingled Cottages at Beach", by 1889
Unidentified
Source: "William R. Emerson," *Illustrated Boston, op. cit.*

"Wyndham," Miss Rose Anne Grosvenor House, 1890
Beacon Hill Road, Newport, Extant
Source: Preservation Society of Newport

"Roslyn," William Grosvenor House, 1901
Harrison Avenue and Beacon Hill Road, Newport, Extant
Source: Preservation Society of Newport

VIRGINIA
Miss Durham House, 1881
Fort Monroe, Not Built or Destroyed
Source: *AABN*, Building Intelligence, January 1, 1881, p. 12